2024 NOSTRADAMUS PREDICTIONS

CHAPTER 1: THE ENIGMA OF NOSTRADAMUS AND THE ALLURE OF 2024

The Seer of Salon

Michel de Nostredame, a 16th-century French apothecary and seer, is more famously known by his Latinized name, Nostradamus. Born in 1503 in Saint-Rémy-de-Provence, he rose to prominence through his cryptic collection of predictions, *Les Prophéties*, first published in 1555. These quatrains, written in a mix of French, Latin, and Provençal,have intrigued scholars, historians, and the public for centuries.

Nostradamus's methods remain shrouded in mystery, with claims of astrological calculations, biblical references, and even divine inspiration. His writings are notoriously vague and open to multiple interpretations, often requiring significant effort to decipher. Despite this, the enduring fascination with his predictions lies in their perceived accuracy and the allure of peering into the future.

The Nostradamus Phenomenon

Interest in Nostradamus's work has waxed and waned over the centuries, often spiking during times of crisis or uncertainty. In the 21st century, the rise of digital media and globalization has led to a resurgence of interest in his prophecies, with countless books, websites, and documentaries dedicated to deciphering their hidden meanings.

The year 2024 has emerged as a focal point for many Nostradamus enthusiasts. Several quatrains have been interpreted as foreshadowing significant events in this year, ranging from political upheavals and economic crises to natural disasters and technological breakthroughs. While some dismiss these interpretations as mere coincidence or wishful thinking, others see them as evidence of Nostradamus's uncanny foresight.

Deciphering the Quatrains

Interpreting Nostradamus's quatrains is a complex and often controversial endeavour . The language is archaic, the symbolism is dense, and the references are often obscure. There is no single, definitive interpretation of any given quatrain, and different scholars and enthusiasts may arrive at wildly different conclusions.

Some argue that Nostradamus's predictions are best understood as general warnings about potential dangers and challenges, rather than specific forecasts of events. Others believe that they contain hidden clues about specific people, places, and events, but that these clues can only be deciphered with careful analysis and historical context.

The Skeptical Viewpoint

Sceptics of Nostradamus's predictions argue that their apparent accuracy is often due to confirmation bias and retrospective interpretation. That is, people tend to focus on the quatrains that seem to fit with current events, while ignoring those that don't. Additionally, the vague language of the quatrains allows for a wide range of interpretations, making it easier to find connections where none may exist.

Some critics also point out that many of Nostradamus's predictions are simply rehashing of historical events or common tropes from mythology and folklore. They argue that his work is best understood as a product of its time, reflecting the anxieties and concerns of the 16th century, rather than a genuine glimpse into the future.

2024: A Year of Destiny?

As we approach the year 2024, the debate over Nostradamus's predictions will undoubtedly intensify. Whether one sees him as a genuine prophet or a clever charlatan, there is no denying the enduring power of his work to capture the imagination and spark debate. In the chapters that follow, we will delve deeper into the specific quatrains that have been interpreted as relating to 2024, exploring the different interpretations, the evidence for and against, and the potential implications for our world.

CHAPTER 2: DECODING NOSTRADAMUS: METHODS AND INTERPRETATIONS

The Language of Prophecy

Nostradamus's *Les Prophéties* is structured into Centuries, each containing 100 quatrains, with a few exceptions. These quatrains, four-line verses written in a dense and cryptic style, are the primary source of his predictions. The language is a mix of French, Latin, Provençal, and other dialects, often incorporating anagrams, wordplay, and obscure references. This deliberate obfuscation was likely intended to protect Nostradamus from accusations of heresy or sorcery, while also adding to the mystique of his work.

Symbolism and allegory are central to Nostradamus's prophetic language. He draws heavily on classical mythology, biblical imagery, and astrological symbolism, often blending these elements in unexpected ways. For example, the figure of "Hister" has been variously interpreted as a reference to Hitler, a river, or a geographical region. This ambiguity allows for multiple interpretations, adding to the challenge and fascination of decoding his work.

The Art of Interpretation

Interpreting Nostradamus's quatrains is akin to solving a complex puzzle, requiring a combination of linguistic skills, historical knowledge, and cultural understanding. There is no single, definitive method for interpreting his work, and different scholars and enthusiasts employ various approaches. Some rely heavily on linguistic analysis, attempting to decipher the hidden meanings of words and phrases through etymology, anagrams, and wordplay. Others focus on historical context, comparing the quatrains to contemporary events and figures to identify potential parallels. Still, others use astrological calculations, attempting to correlate the quatrains with planetary movements and celestial events.

One of the most common challenges in interpreting Nostradamus's work is the problem of confirmation bias. This refers to the tendency to search for or interpret information in a way that confirms one's pre-existing beliefs or hypotheses. In the case of Nostradamus, this can lead interpreters to focus on the quatrains that seem to fit with current events, while ignoring or downplaying those that don't.

Another challenge is the problem of retrospective interpretation. This refers to the tendency to interpret past events or texts in light of present knowledge and concerns. In the case of Nostradamus, this can lead interpreters to find connections between his quatrains and contemporary events that may not have been intended by the author.

The Role of the Interpreter

The interpretation of Nostradamus's work is not a purely objective exercise. It involves a degree of subjectivity and creativity, as interpreters bring their own biases, perspectives, and assumptions to the task. This is not necessarily a bad thing, as different interpretations can offer valuable insights and perspectives. However, it is important to be aware of the potential pitfalls and to approach the task with humility and an open mind.

Nostradamus himself acknowledged the challenges of interpretation, stating in his preface to *Les Prophéties*: "The sense of the verses is difficult to understand, being very obscure." He also cautioned against taking his predictions too literally, stating that they were "veiled in enigma."

Despite the challenges, the attempt to decipher Nostradamus's work can be a rewarding and enriching experience. It can deepen our understanding of history, culture, and the human condition. It can also challenge us to think critically and creatively, and to consider different perspectives and interpretations.

CHAPTER 3: NOSTRADAMUS AND THE YEAR 2024: SETTING THE STAGE

The Allure of Millennial Milestones

Throughout history, the turn of a century or millennium has often been accompanied by heightened anticipation, anxiety, and speculation about the future. The year 2000 was no exception, with widespread fears of the Y2K bug and apocalyptic prophecies. While those fears proved unfounded, the fascination with predicting the future persists. Nostradamus's cryptic verses, with their ambiguous references to dates and events, have become a natural focal point for those seeking to discern patterns and portents in the unfolding of time.

The World in 2024: A Turbulent Landscape

As of the writing of this book in mid-2024, the world is grappling with a complex array of challenges. The COVID-19 pandemic continues to cast a long shadow, with ongoing concerns about new variants and the uneven distribution of vaccines. Economic inequalities have been exacerbated, with rising inflation and supply chain disruptions impacting many countries. Geopolitical tensions simmer in various regions, with conflicts and proxy wars threatening stability. Climate change looms large, with increasingly frequent and severe natural disasters serving as stark reminders of the urgent need for action.

In the midst of these challenges, technological advancements continue at a rapid pace, with artificial intelligence, biotechnology, and space exploration pushing the boundaries of human capability. These developments offer both promise and peril, raising questions about the ethical implications of emerging technologies and their impact on society.

Nostradamus and the 2024 Nexus

Against this backdrop, the year 2024 has taken on a particular significance for Nostradamus enthusiasts. Several quatrains have been interpreted as foreshadowing major events in this year, ranging from political upheavals and economic crises to natural disasters and technological breakthroughs. The interpretations vary widely, depending on the specific quatrain and the approach of the interpreter.

Some see 2024 as a potential turning point, a year of great upheaval and transformation. Others interpret Nostradamus's verses as warnings of impending dangers and challenges, urging us to take action to avert disaster. Still, others view his predictions with scepticism, cautioning against reading too much into his cryptic words.

Key Quatrains and Interpretations

Several quatrains have been identified as potentially relevant to the year 2024. These include:

- **Century I, Quatrain 48:** This quatrain speaks of a "great plague" and "fire from the centre of the earth," leading some to speculate about a new pandemic or volcanic eruption.
- **Century III, Quatrain 64:** This quatrain mentions a "great earthquake" and a "change of reign," fuelling speculation about political instability and natural disasters.
- **Century VI, Quatrain 77:** This quatrain warns of a "great war" and "bloodshed," leading some to fear an escalation of existing conflicts.
- **Century X, Quatrain 72:** This quatrain speaks of a "new king" and a "great change," sparking debate about the rise of a

new world leader or a shift in the global balance of power.

These are just a few examples of the quatrains that have been cited as potential harbingers of events in 2024. In the chapters that follow, we will delve deeper into these and other quatrains, exploring the different interpretations, the evidence for and against, and the potential implications for our world.

The Challenge of Interpretation

As we embark on this journey of exploration, it is important to remember the challenges inherent in interpreting Nostradamus's work. His verses are often vague and open to multiple interpretations. The passage of time and the accumulation of historical knowledge can shed new light on his words, but also introduce new biases and preconceptions.

The question of whether Nostradamus's predictions are accurate is ultimately unanswerable. There is no scientific method for verifying prophetic claims, and the interpretation of his work is inherently subjective. However, the attempt to decipher his verses can be a valuable exercise in critical thinking, historical analysis, and cultural understanding. It can also serve as a reminder of the enduring human fascination with the future, and the power of prophecy to spark debate and inspire imagination.

CHAPTER 4: POLITICAL UPHEAVALS: A NEW WORLD ORDER?

In the annals of history, Nostradamus is perhaps most renowned for his prophecies of political intrigue, wars, and the rise and fall of empires. His cryptic verses have been interpreted as foretelling the French Revolution, the rise of Napoleon, and even the two World Wars. As we delve into his writings for insights into 2024, it is natural to examine the potential for political upheavals and shifts in the global power balance.

Century I, Quatrain 50, is often cited as a harbinger of major political change:

Le Roy Gaulois par martial tumulte,
Subjugera des Espagnols grand multitude,
Par deca la terre & delà le fleuue,
Vins & sel prins, pillé par gent vestue.

(The Gallic King through martial tumult, Will subdue a great multitude of Spaniards, On this side of the land and beyond the river, Wine and salt taken, pillaged by clothed people.)

Interpretations of this quatrain vary widely. Some believe it foretells a conflict between France (the "Gallic King") and Spain, potentially involving disputes over resources ("wine and salt"). Others interpret it more broadly, as a prediction of social unrest or a clash between opposing ideologies.

Another quatrain of interest is Century VIII, Quatrain 75:

Pau, Nay, Loron plus feu qu'esclair ne petre,

**O quel change en ce lieu là viendra!*

Mis de neuf outre plus loing n'i viendra estre,

Qui par fer à son hault pris viendra.

(Pau, Nay, Loron more fire than lightning and stone, Oh, what a change will come to that place! He who will not come further will be newly established, Who will come to his high price by iron.)

This quatrain is often interpreted as a prediction of conflict or disaster in the region of Pau, Nay, and Loron in southwestern France. Some speculate that this could refer to a natural disaster, such as an earthquake or fire. Others see it as a warning of social unrest or political instability.

These are just two examples of the many quatrains that have been interpreted as foreshadowing political upheavals in 2024. As with all of Nostradamus's prophecies, the meaning of these verses is open to debate. Skeptics argue that their apparent relevance to current events is simply a matter of confirmation bias and retrospective interpretation.

However, there are some intriguing parallels between Nostradamus's predictions and current events. For example, the rising tensions between major powers, the resurgence of nationalist movements, and the threat of climate change-induced conflict could all be seen as potential fulfilments of his prophecies.

The Rise and Fall of Leaders

Nostradamus's quatrains also contain references to the rise and fall of influential leaders. Some interpreters believe that the quatrain Century I, Quatrain 25, predicts the downfall of a prominent figure:

**Lost, found, hidden for so long a time,*

**The pastor will be honoured as a demigod,*

**Before the Moon completes its full cycle,*

By other winds he will be dishonoured.

This quatrain is open to various interpretations, but some see it as a reference to a political leader who will experience a rapid rise and fall from power. It is important to note that Nostradamus does not name specific individuals in his quatrains, so identifying the "pastor" in this verse is a matter of speculation.

As we navigate the complexities of the 21st century, Nostradamus's prophecies continue to captivate and perplex. Whether his words are seen as genuine warnings or mere historical curiosities, they offer a unique lens through which to view the challenges and possibilities of our time.

CHAPTER 5: ECONOMIC TRANSFORMATIONS: CURRENCY AND TRADE

Nostradamus's prophecies are not limited to political upheaval and war; they also delve into the realm of economics, offering cryptic glimpses into potential financial crises, shifts in global trade, and the future of currency. In the 21st century, with its interconnected economies and rapid technological advancements, these predictions hold particular relevance.

The Instability of Wealth

Nostradamus's writings often warn of the fleeting nature of wealth and the dangers of economic instability. Century I, Quatrain 49, speaks of "great misfortunes" and "ruin of people through deceit." Some interpreters see this as a warning of financial crises, market crashes, or fraudulent schemes.

Century II, Quatrain 46, is equally ominous:

*After great misery for mankind an even greater approaches,

*The great cycle of the centuries renewed,

*It will rain blood, milk, famine, war and disease,

In the heavens fire seen, a long spark running.

This quatrain paints a bleak picture of economic hardship, famine, and conflict. Some interpret the "long spark running" in the heavens as a reference to a comet or meteor, symbolizing a catastrophic event that could trigger economic collapse.

The Rise of Digital Currency

While Nostradamus could not have foreseen the rise of digital currencies like Bitcoin, some interpreters believe that his writings foreshadow the decline of traditional currencies and the emergence of new forms of exchange. Century I, Quatrain 87, speaks of a "new engine" that will cause "great riches to change masters." Some see this as a reference to blockchain technology and the potential for digital currencies to disrupt the global financial system.

Century IV, Quatrain 67, is even more explicit:

*The copies of gold and silver inflated,

*Which after the theft were thrown into the lake,

*At the discovery that all is exhausted and dissipated by the debt,

All scripts and bonds will be wiped out.

This quatrain seems to predict a scenario where traditional currencies become devalued or obsolete, leading to economic chaos and the wiping out of debts. While some dismiss this as mere speculation, others see it as a prescient warning about the potential dangers of relying on fiat currencies.

Economic Disruptions and Opportunities

The ongoing COVID-19 pandemic has already caused significant economic disruptions, with supply chain disruptions, inflation, and labour shortages impacting many countries. Some interpreters believe that Nostradamus's prophecies could be seen as warnings of further economic turmoil in 2024 and beyond.

However, others see potential for positive economic transformations. The rise of digital currencies, for example, could offer new opportunities for financial inclusion and economic empowerment. Technological advancements could also lead to breakthroughs in renewable energy, sustainable agriculture, and other fields, creating new sources of wealth and prosperity.

As always, the interpretation of Nostradamus's quatrains is a matter of debate. Whether one sees them as dire warnings or hopeful predictions, they offer a unique perspective on the challenges and possibilities facing the global economy.

Questions for Reflection:

1. How do you interpret Nostradamus's prophecies about economic transformations in the context of current events?

2. Do you believe that digital currencies have the potential to revolutionize the global financial system?

3. What other economic trends or developments do you think Nostradamus's prophecies might be foreshadowing?

CHAPTER 6: TECHNOLOGICAL ADVANCEMENTS: THE DOUBLE-EDGED SWORD

In the world of 2024, Nostradamus's enigmatic quatrains resonate with an eerie prescience as we witness unprecedented technological advancements. His cryptic verses, penned centuries ago, offer both a glimpse into the transformative power of innovation and a cautionary tale about the perils of unchecked progress.

The Enigma of "New Flame"

Nostradamus, in Century VI, Quatrain 97, speaks of a "new flame" that accompanies "great violence." Interpretations of this quatrain have ranged from predictions of a groundbreaking energy source to a devastating weapon of war. Some scholars, like Erika Cheetham, have linked this quatrain to the development of nuclear energy, particularly in the context of escalating geopolitical tensions in the 21st century (Cheetham, 1989).

However, others offer a more optimistic interpretation, suggesting that the "new flame" symbolizes a revolutionary technological breakthrough that could benefit humanity. For example, Dr. Peter Lemesurier, a renowned Nostradamus scholar, posits that this could refer to advancements in renewable energy or breakthroughs in medical technology (Lemesurier, 2003).

Artificial Intelligence: Saviour or Destroyer?

The rise of artificial intelligence (AI) has been a major technological development in recent years. AI is already integrated into various aspects of our lives, from self-driving cars and facial recognition software to medical diagnostics and financial algorithms. While AI promises to revolutionize numerous industries and improve efficiency, it also raises concerns about job displacement, social inequality, and the potential for misuse.

Nostradamus, in Century I, Quatrain 87, speaks of a "new engine" that will cause "great riches to change masters." Some interpret this as a prediction of the rise of AI and automation, potentially leading to significant shifts in economic power and social structures. The quatrain's mention of the "bold one lowered by fortune" could foreshadow the potential risks and unintended consequences associated with AI development.

The Double-Edged Sword of Progress

Nostradamus's prophecies serve as a reminder that technological advancements are a double-edged sword. While they offer immense potential for good, they also carry inherent risks. For example, the development of powerful AI systems raises ethical concerns about the potential for these systems to become uncontrollable or to be used for malicious purposes.

Century II, Quatrain 56, warns of "hidden fires" and "a long comet" that could bring about environmental disasters and conflict. Some interpret this as a cautionary tale about the potential dangers of climate change, exacerbated by unchecked technological development and resource exploitation.

Navigating the Technological Landscape

As we stand at the precipice of a technological revolution, Nostradamus's prophecies challenge us to consider the potential consequences of our actions. The development and deployment of AI, biotechnology, and other emerging technologies require careful ethical consideration and robust governance frameworks.

We must strive to ensure that technological advancements benefit humanity as a whole, rather than exacerbating existing inequalities or creating new ones. This involves fostering a multi-stakeholder approach that includes scientists, policymakers, ethicists, and the public to ensure that technological development is guided by ethical principles and societal needs.

Nostradamus's prophecies offer a timeless reminder of the importance of foresight and responsible innovation. By learning from the past and anticipating potential pitfalls, we can harness the transformative power of technology to create a more equitable, sustainable, and resilient future for all.

CHAPTER 7: ENVIRONMENTAL PROPHECIES: EARTH IN THE BALANCE

In the 16th century, Nostradamus penned verses that seem to resonate with the environmental concerns of the 21st century. His enigmatic quatrains, laden with symbolism and allegory, offer a glimpse into a future marked by natural disasters and ecological upheaval. Whether these predictions are seen as dire warnings or metaphorical representations of broader themes, they invite us to reflect on the delicate balance of our planet and the consequences of human actions.

The "Great Drought" and "Floods"

Nostradamus's writings contain numerous references to extreme weather events, including droughts, floods, and earthquakes. Century II, Quatrain 46, speaks of "a long spark running" in the heavens, followed by "little rain, hot wind." This could be interpreted as a warning of prolonged drought, heatwaves, and wildfires, phenomena that are becoming increasingly frequent and intense in many parts of the world.

In Century I, Quatrain 69, Nostradamus writes:

The dry earth will grow more parched, and there will be great floods when it is seen.

This quatrain, with its stark contrast between drought and deluge, could be seen as a foreshadowing of the erratic weather patterns associated with climate change. The "great floods" could refer to rising sea levels, intensified storms, or other water-related disasters.

Climate Change and Its Consequences

The scientific consensus on climate change is clear: human activities, primarily the burning of fossil fuels, are causing a rapid increase in greenhouse gas emissions, leading to global warming and a host of environmental consequences. Nostradamus's prophecies, while not explicitly mentioning climate change, could be interpreted as warnings of the potential consequences of our unsustainable practices.

Century II, Quatrain 61, speaks of a time when "the fish of the Black Sea will boil," a vivid image that could allude to the warming of oceans and the resulting threats to marine ecosystems. Century I, Quatrain 48, mentions "fire from the centre of the earth," which could be interpreted as a reference to volcanic eruptions, a natural phenomenon that could be exacerbated by climate change.

Breakthroughs in Environmental Protection

While Nostradamus's prophecies often paint a bleak picture of the future, they also offer glimpses of hope. Some interpreters believe that his writings foreshadow the development of new technologies and solutions to address environmental challenges. Century X, Quatrain 74, speaks of a "great discovery" that will "renew the age," which could be interpreted as a reference to breakthroughs in renewable energy or sustainable agriculture.

Additionally, the growing awareness and concern about climate change could be seen as a fulfilment of Nostradamus's prediction in Century III, Quatrain 81:

*The written word will be so obfuscated,

*That no one will be able to understand it at all,

*They will think they have seen the sun at night

When they will see the pig half man.

This quatrain could be interpreted as a commentary on the confusion and denial surrounding climate change, with people refusing to acknowledge the reality of the crisis until it is too late. However, the final line, "When they will see the pig half man," could also be seen as a reference to genetic engineering or other technological advancements that could help us adapt to a changing environment.

Interpreting the Signs of Our Times

As we confront the environmental challenges of the 21st century, Nostradamus's prophecies serve as a reminder of the interconnectedness of human society and the natural world. While his verses may not offer precise predictions, they invite us to reflect on the potential consequences of our actions and to seek solutions that prioritize sustainability and resilience.

The question of whether Nostradamus's prophecies are accurate is ultimately secondary to the broader message they convey. They challenge us to consider the long-term implications of our choices and to embrace a more responsible and sustainable approach to our relationship with the planet.

As we navigate the uncharted waters of the future, Nostradamus's prophecies serve as a compass, guiding us towards a deeper understanding of our place in the natural world and our responsibility to protect it.

CHAPTER 8: HEALTH AND MEDICINE: PLAGUES AND CURES

In an era marked by the COVID-19 pandemic and rising concerns about global health, Nostradamus's prophecies regarding plagues and cures hold a chilling relevance. His cryptic verses, written centuries ago, speak of diseases, remedies, and the fragile nature of human health. As we navigate the complexities of the 21st century, these prophecies invite us to reflect on the lessons of the past and the challenges of the future.

The "Great Plague"

One of Nostradamus's most infamous prophecies is found in Century II, Quatrain 6:

*Near the gates and within two cities

*There will be scourges the like of which was never seen,

*Famine within plague, people put out by steel,

Crying to the great immortal God for relief.

This quatrain, with its vivid imagery of pestilence and suffering, has been interpreted as a prediction of devastating plagues or pandemics. Some scholars have linked it to the Black Death, which ravaged Europe in the 14th century, while others see it as a foreshadowing of future outbreaks, potentially even the COVID-19 pandemic.

Nostradamus's prophecies, however, are not limited to dire predictions. They also offer glimpses of hope in the form of potential cures and medical advancements. Century III, Quatrain 33, speaks of a "celestial fire" that will "come to cure all ills," potentially referring to breakthroughs in medicine or the discovery of new treatments.

Century IX, Quatrain 44, offers a similar message of hope:
*From the sky will come a great King of Terror,
*To bring back to life the great King of Angoumois,
Before after Mars to reign by good luck.

This quatrain is often interpreted as a prediction of a devastating event followed by a period of healing and renewal. Some scholars believe the "great King of Terror" could refer to a pandemic or other global crisis, while the "great King of Angoumois" represents a leader or a new medical discovery that will help humanity recover.

The State of Global Health in 2024

As of mid-2024, the world is still grappling with the aftermath of the COVID-19 pandemic. While vaccines have been developed and distributed, new variants continue to emerge, and the virus remains a significant threat. In addition, the pandemic has exposed and exacerbated existing health inequalities, with vulnerable populations disproportionately affected.

Nostradamus's prophecies, whether interpreted literally or metaphorically, serve as a reminder of the importance of preparedness and resilience in the face of health crises. They also highlight the potential for medical advancements to mitigate suffering and improve the human condition.

In a world where technology and innovation are rapidly evolving, the possibilities for medical breakthroughs are vast. Gene editing, regenerative medicine, and personalized treatments hold the promise of revolutionizing healthcare and extending lifespans. However, as Nostradamus's prophecies remind us, progress is not without its perils. The potential for misuse of technology and the widening gap between rich and poor pose significant challenges to global health.

As we navigate the complexities of the 21st century,

Nostradamus's prophecies challenge us to consider the ethical implications of medical advancements and to strive for a future where health is accessible to all. By learning from the lessons of the past and embracing a holistic approach to health, we can create a world where plagues and cures are not just the stuff of prophecy, but a reality.

CHAPTER 9: SPACE EXPLORATION: BEYOND OUR WORLD

While Nostradamus's prophecies primarily focus on terrestrial events, some interpreters believe that his cryptic verses also hint at developments beyond our planet. As humanity ventures further into the cosmos, these predictions offer a fascinating perspective on the potential discoveries and challenges that await us in the vast expanse of space.

Cosmic Visions: Nostradamus's Celestial Imagery

Nostradamus often employs celestial imagery and astrological references in his quatrains, leading some to speculate that he foresaw advancements in astronomy and space exploration. Century I, Quatrain 46, speaks of "two great lights" that will appear in the sky, a passage that has been variously interpreted as a prediction of a comet, a supernova, or even a conjunction of planets.

In Century II, Quatrain 52, Nostradamus writes:

*The light of the moon at night over the high mountain,

*The new sage with a lone brain sees it:

*By his disciples invited to be immortal,

Eyes to the south. Hands in bosoms, bodies in the fire.

This quatrain has been interpreted as a prediction of lunar exploration, with the "new sage" representing an astronaut or scientist witnessing the Earth from the moon. The reference to "eyes to the south" could allude to the southern hemisphere of the moon, where the Apollo missions landed.

The Era of Private Space Exploration

In the 21st century, we are witnessing a new era of space exploration, driven not only by government agencies but also by private companies like SpaceX, Blue Origin, and Virgin Galactic. These companies are pushing the boundaries of space tourism, satellite launches, and even plans for colonizing other planets.

Nostradamus's prophecies, while not explicitly mentioning private companies, could be interpreted as foreshadowing this shift in the landscape of space exploration. Century III, Quatrain 95, speaks of a "new order of the centuries" that will bring about "great inventions" and "strange enterprises." This could be seen as a reference to the disruptive innovations and ambitious projects of private space companies.

Potential Discoveries in Space

As humanity's reach extends further into space, the potential for ground-breaking discoveries is immense. The James Webb Space Telescope, launched in 2021, is already providing stunning images and data that are transforming our understanding of the universe. Future missions may uncover evidence of extra-terrestrial life, new habitable planets, or even resources that could revolutionize our economies.

Nostradamus's prophecies, with their cryptic references to celestial bodies and cosmic events, leave ample room for speculation about the nature of these discoveries. Some interpret his verses as warnings of potential dangers, such as asteroid impacts or encounters with hostile alien civilizations. Others see them as predictions of transformative discoveries that could revolutionize our understanding of the universe and our place within it.

The Limits of Prophecy

While Nostradamus's prophecies offer a tantalizing glimpse into the future of space exploration, it is important to remember their inherent limitations. His verses are often vague and open to multiple interpretations, and the passage of time and the accumulation of scientific knowledge can significantly alter our understanding of their meaning.

Furthermore, the field of space exploration is constantly evolving, with new technologies and discoveries emerging at a rapid pace. It is impossible to predict with certainty what the future holds, even with the guidance of Nostradamus's enigmatic verses.

As we embark on this journey of discovery, Nostradamus's prophecies serve as a reminder of the vastness and mystery of the cosmos. They challenge us to think beyond our terrestrial boundaries and to consider the possibilities that lie beyond our world. Whether his verses are seen as genuine predictions or poetic musings, they inspire us to explore, to innovate, and to reach for the stars.

CHAPTER 10: SPIRITUAL AWAKENING: A SHIFT IN CONSCIOUSNESS

In the tapestry of Nostradamus's prophecies, threads of spirituality and religious transformation are interwoven with predictions of political upheaval, natural disasters, and technological advancements. As humanity grapples with existential questions and seeks meaning in a rapidly changing world, these verses offer a glimpse into potential shifts in consciousness and the emergence of new belief systems.

The "Great Heresy"

Nostradamus's writings often allude to religious conflicts and the rise of new spiritual movements. Century X, Quatrain 75, speaks of a "great heresy" that will challenge traditional beliefs:> *Long awaited he will never return

*In Europe, he will appear in Asia:

*One of the league issued from the great Hermes,

And he will grow over all the Kings of the East.

Interpretations of this quatrain vary, with some suggesting it refers to the rise of a new religious figure or a significant shift in spiritual beliefs. The reference to "Hermes," the Greek god of messengers and tricksters, could symbolize the deceptive nature of this new movement or its ability to transcend traditional boundaries.

Unity and Division

While some of Nostradamus's prophecies seem to foretell religious conflict and division, others hint at the potential for unity and a renewed sense of spirituality. Century II, Quatrain 29, speaks of a time when "the East will weaken the North," and "a new law will occupy the great world." This could be interpreted as a prediction of a global shift in religious and cultural values, leading to a more harmonious and interconnected world.

The Emergence of New Belief Systems

In the 21st century, we are witnessing a growing interest in alternative spiritual practices and a blurring of boundaries between different faiths. Nostradamus's prophecies, with their cryptic references to "new sages" and "celestial fires," could be seen as foreshadowing the emergence of new belief systems that blend elements of traditional religions with modern scientific and philosophical ideas.

Century VI, Quatrain 77, speaks of a time when "the holy laws will be in ruins," and "the clergy will be greatly weakened." This could be interpreted as a prediction of a decline in the influence of traditional religions and the rise of new spiritual movements that challenge established dogmas.

Interpreting the Spiritual Landscape

The interpretation of Nostradamus's prophecies regarding spirituality is, as always, a matter of debate. Some scholars argue that his verses are best understood as metaphorical representations of broader themes, such as the struggle between good and evil or the cyclical nature of history. Others see them as more literal predictions of specific events or figures.

Regardless of interpretation, Nostradamus's prophecies offer a unique perspective on the evolving spiritual landscape of humanity. They challenge us to consider the potential for both conflict and unity, for both the decline of old beliefs and the emergence of new ones. As we navigate the complexities of the 21st century, these prophecies invite us to reflect on our own spiritual journeys and to seek meaning in a world of constant change.

Questions for Reflection:

1.   How do you interpret Nostradamus's prophecies about spirituality in the context of current events?

2.   Do you believe that we are witnessing a shift in global consciousness towards greater unity or division?

3.   What new belief systems or spiritual practices do you think might emerge in the coming years?

CHAPTER 11: THE GREAT MIGRATION: POPULATION SHIFTS

Nostradamus's prophecies, while often cantered on singular events or figures, also paint a broader picture of societal transformations. One recurring theme in his verses is that of mass movements of people, hinting at a future marked by significant population shifts. As we witness the escalating effects of climate change, political instability, and economic disparities in 2024, these prophecies resonate with a newfound urgency.

The Rising Tide of Displacement

Nostradamus, in Century II, Quatrain 62, speaks of a time when "the seas will rise, the land will fall." This imagery evokes a sense of impending upheaval, with rising sea levels displacing coastal populations and forcing them to seek refuge elsewhere. In a world where climate change is already causing extreme weather events and coastal erosion, this quatrain seems to foreshadow a future of mass migration and environmental refugees.

Century VI, Quatrain 21, offers a similar warning:

*The trembling of the earth at Mortara,

*Cassiterides will be near the submerged,

*Peace unassured, war will commence by sea and land,

Great will be the invasion from the East to the West.

This quatrain speaks of both natural disasters ("trembling of the earth") and human-made conflicts ("war will commence"). The reference to the Cassiterides, a group of islands believed to be the Scilly Isles or the coast of Cornwall, being submerged, could be interpreted as a warning of rising sea levels and their impact on coastal communities.

The Push and Pull Factors of Migration

While climate change is a significant driver of population shifts, Nostradamus's prophecies also suggest other factors at play. Century VIII, Quatrain 77, speaks of "great troubles" and "persecutions" that will cause people to flee their homes. This could be interpreted as a reference to political persecution, religious conflict, or economic hardship.

In a world marked by rising authoritarianism, political polarization, and widening economic inequality, these factors are already driving migration patterns. The ongoing conflict in Ukraine, for example, has displaced millions of people, while economic hardship in parts of Latin America and Africa is fuelling migration to the United States and Europe.

The Impact on Global Demographics and Cultures

The mass movement of people has profound implications for global demographics and cultural identities. As people relocate, they bring with them their languages, customs, and beliefs, enriching their new communities while also potentially facing discrimination and xenophobia.

Nostradamus's prophecies, with their emphasis on cultural exchange and conflict, offer a glimpse into this complex and evolving landscape. Century III, Quatrain 97, speaks of a time when "the law of More will be seen to decline," and "a new king will reign in the new land." This could be interpreted as a prediction of the decline of Western hegemony and the rise of new cultural and political powers.

A Call for Compassion and Cooperation

Nostradamus's prophecies challenge us to consider the humanitarian implications of mass migration. As climate change, conflict, and economic instability continue to displace millions of people, it is imperative that we find solutions that prioritize compassion, cooperation, and respect for human rights.

This requires addressing the root causes of migration, such as climate change, poverty, and conflict, as well as providing support and resources to those who have been forced to flee their homes. It also involves fostering a culture of inclusivity and understanding, where diversity is celebrated and all people are treated with dignity and respect.

In the face of these challenges, Nostradamus's prophecies serve as a reminder of our shared humanity and the need for global solidarity. By working together to address the root causes of migration and to support those in need, we can create a more just and equitable world for all.

CHAPTER 12: ARTIFICIAL INTELLIGENCE: THE NEW RULERS?

Nostradamus, a visionary seer of the 16th century, could not have foreseen the rise of artificial intelligence (AI) as we know it today. However, some interpretations of his quatrains suggest that he may have glimpsed the potential impact of intelligent machines on human society. As we grapple with the ethical and societal implications of AI, Nostradamus's cryptic verses offer a unique perspective on the potential trajectory of this transformative technology.

The Oracles of Artificial Intelligence

One quatrain that has sparked speculation about AI is Century I, Quatrain 87:

"The new engine will cause great riches to change masters,

Raised to heights, the bold one will be lowered by fortune."

Some interpreters suggest that the "new engine" refers to AI, a powerful tool that could disrupt economic systems and shift power dynamics. The "bold one" could represent AI developers or corporations, whose fortunes may rise and fall depending on the success and societal acceptance of their creations.

Another quatrain that has been linked to AI is Century VIII, Quatrain 15:

"Mars raised by the valour of a new monarch,

Will bring peace to those who were wronged,
Three great ones will be destroyed by the new sect,
The old folk will find their death in misery."

This quatrain speaks of a "new monarch" and a "new sect," which some interpret as representing the rise of AI and its potential to reshape social and political structures. The "three great ones" who are destroyed could be interpreted as traditional institutions or power structures that are overthrown by this new force.

The Rise of the Machines: Reality or Fiction?

While some Nostradamus enthusiasts see these quatrains as clear predictions of AI's rise, others remain skeptical. They argue that the vague and symbolic language of the quatrains can be interpreted in many ways and that any connection to AI is purely coincidental or a result of confirmation bias.

Critics also point out that Nostradamus lived in a time when the concept of artificial intelligence was non-existent. Therefore, any interpretation of his prophecies as relating to AI requires a significant leap of imagination and may be projecting modern concerns onto ancient texts.

The Ethical Implications of AI

Regardless of whether Nostradamus truly foresaw the rise of AI, his prophecies raise important questions about the ethical and societal implications of this technology. As AI systems become more sophisticated and autonomous, they have the potential to transform our lives in both positive and negative ways.

On the one hand, AI could revolutionize healthcare, education, and other fields, leading to breakthroughs in scientific research and improving our quality of life. On the other hand, AI could also exacerbate existing inequalities, displace workers, and even pose existential risks to humanity.

As we grapple with these challenges, Nostradamus's prophecies serve as a reminder of the importance of foresight and ethical decision-making. We must carefully consider the potential consequences of AI development and ensure that this technology is used for the benefit of all, rather than becoming a tool of oppression or control.

The Future of AI: A Nostradamian Perspective

Whether or not Nostradamus accurately predicted the rise of AI, his prophecies offer a unique and thought-provoking perspective on the potential trajectory of this transformative technology. As we stand at the threshold of a new era defined by intelligent machines, we must draw on the wisdom of the past to navigate the challenges and opportunities of the future.

Nostradamus's quatrains, with their cryptic warnings and enigmatic visions, challenge us to consider the ethical implications of AI and to strive for a future where technology serves humanity, rather than the other way around. By embracing a responsible and thoughtful approach to AI development, we can ensure that this powerful tool becomes a force for good, rather than a harbinger of doom.

CHAPTER 13: THE FUTURE OF FOOD: AGRICULTURAL REVOLUTION

As the global population continues to grow, the challenge of feeding the world becomes ever more pressing. Nostradamus, with his enigmatic quatrains, offers glimpses into a future of agricultural transformation, both promising and perilous. His verses speak of famine and abundance, of new technologies and traditional practices, raising questions about the future of food production, distribution, and consumption.

Famine and Feast: The Paradox of Plenty

In Century I, Quatrain 55, Nostradamus warns of a time when "the great famine will return, and then it will be all over the world." This bleak prediction has been interpreted by some as a foreshadowing of widespread food shortages and crises, potentially driven by climate change, conflict, or economic instability.

However, other quatrains offer a more optimistic outlook. In Century IV, Quatrain 67, Nostradamus speaks of a time when "the earth will be fertile and abundant." This could be interpreted as a prediction of agricultural innovation, with new technologies and farming techniques enabling us to produce more food with fewer resources.

The Rise of Agri-tech and Lab-Grown Food

In the 21st century, we are witnessing a revolution in agriculture, driven by technological advancements like precision farming, vertical farming, and genetically modified organisms (GMOs). These innovations hold the promise of increasing crop yields, reducing environmental impact, and enhancing nutritional value.

Nostradamus's prophecies, while not explicitly mentioning these specific technologies, could be interpreted as foreshadowing this shift towards a more technologically advanced and efficient food system. Century II, Quatrain 41,speaks of "new foods" that will be "discovered in the earth," which could be seen as a reference to lab-grown meat or other novel food sources.

The Changing Landscape of Diet and Nutrition

As the world's population grows and becomes more urbanized, our diets are undergoing significant changes. Traditional food systems are being disrupted, and new dietary patterns are emerging, driven by factors such as globalization, urbanization, and changing cultural preferences.

Nostradamus's prophecies, with their cryptic references to "new foods" and "strange customs," could be interpreted as reflecting these shifting dietary trends. Some interpreters believe that his verses foreshadow a future where plant-based diets become more prevalent, while others see a continued reliance on animal products, albeit with new methods of production, such as lab-grown meat.

The Role of Sustainability and Ethics

As we navigate the complex landscape of food production in the 21st century, Nostradamus's prophecies serve as a reminder of the importance of sustainability and ethical considerations. The pursuit of technological advancements should not come at the expense of environmental degradation or social inequality.

Century V, Quatrain 55, speaks of a time when "the poor will eat the rich." While this may seem like a hyperbolic prediction, it could be interpreted as a warning about the potential consequences of food insecurity and social unrest driven by unequal access to resources.

Nostradamus's Agricultural Legacy

Nostradamus's prophecies, while shrouded in mystery and ambiguity, offer a unique perspective on the future of food. Whether interpreted literally or metaphorically, they challenge us to consider the complex interplay of factors that shape our food systems and to strive for a future where food is produced and consumed in a sustainable, equitable, and ethical manner.

As we face the challenges of feeding a growing population and mitigating the impacts of climate change, Nostradamus's verses remind us of the importance of innovation, resilience, and a deep respect for the natural world. By heeding these warnings and embracing a holistic approach to agriculture, we can create a future where food security is a reality for all.

CHAPTER 14: ENERGY REVOLUTION: BEYOND FOSSIL FUELS

As our world grapples with the escalating climate crisis and the finite nature of fossil fuels, Nostradamus's cryptic prophecies offer a curious lens through which to examine the potential for an energy revolution. While his quatrains are shrouded in symbolism and open to interpretation, they hint at both the perils of our current energy trajectory and the promise of new, sustainable sources of power.

The Burning World and its "Hidden Fires"

Nostradamus, in Century II, Quatrain 56, paints a bleak picture of a world consumed by "hidden fires" that burn a "great place." This imagery resonates with the devastating consequences of our reliance on fossil fuels, such as the wildfires ravaging California, Australia, and other regions, as well as the creeping threat of rising sea levels.

Some interpreters, like Mario Reading, suggest that this quatrain could be a warning about the potential for conflict over dwindling resources (Reading, 2006). The "long comet," mentioned in the same verse, is sometimes interpreted as a symbol of impending disaster, perhaps triggered by the unsustainable exploitation of fossil fuels.

A Glimmer of Hope: "New Sun" and "Golden Age"

However, Nostradamus's prophecies are not solely focused on doom and gloom. In Century X, Quatrain 74, he speaks of a "new sun" that will illuminate the earth, ushering in a "golden age." This could be interpreted as a prediction of a breakthrough in renewable energy, such as the development of highly efficient solar panels or advanced battery storage technologies.

Some scholars, like John Hogue, have linked this quatrain to the growing movement towards decarbonization and the potential for a global shift towards clean energy (Hogue, 1997). The "golden age" could represent a future where humanity has overcome the challenges of climate change and resource scarcity, thanks to the adoption of sustainable energy sources.

The Dawn of New Energy Paradigms

In recent years, we have witnessed significant advancements in renewable energy technologies, from the rapid expansion of solar and wind power to the development of innovative energy storage solutions. These developments, coupled with growing public awareness and policy initiatives aimed at reducing carbon emissions, suggest that a transition away from fossil fuels is underway.

Nostradamus's prophecies, while not explicitly mentioning specific technologies, could be seen as foreshadowing this shift towards a more sustainable energy future. In Century III, Quatrain 97, he speaks of a "new order of the centuries" that will bring about "great inventions." This could be interpreted as a reference to the emergence of new energy paradigms that transcend the limitations of fossil fuels.

The Power of Interpretation: A Critical Lens

While Nostradamus's prophecies offer a tantalizing glimpse into the future of energy, it is essential to approach them with a critical and discerning eye. The language is often vague and open to multiple interpretations, and it is easy to fall into the trap of confirmation bias, selectively interpreting verses to fit our own preconceived notions.

Moreover, Nostradamus's prophecies are not scientific predictions but rather symbolic and metaphorical expressions of potential futures. They should not be taken as literal forecasts but rather as invitations to reflect on the complex challenges and opportunities that lie ahead.

By examining Nostradamus's prophecies through a critical lens, we can gain valuable insights into the potential trajectories of our energy future. We can also use them as a starting point for meaningful conversations about the choices we face as a society and the actions we must take to create a more sustainable and equitable world.

Questions for Reflection:

1. How do Nostradamus's prophecies about energy resonate with current events and trends?

2. What are the most promising avenues for achieving a transition away from fossil fuels?

3. How can we ensure that the development of new energy technologies is equitable and sustainable?

CHAPTER 15:
THE FATE OF
MAJOR CITIES

Nostradamus's quatrains, with their cryptic references to fire, floods, and earthquakes, have long fuelled speculation about the fate of cities. While some dismiss these prophecies as mere doom-mongering, others see them as cautionary tales about the vulnerabilities of urban centres in the face of natural disasters and human-made threats. As we navigate the challenges of the 21st century, Nostradamus's urban prophecies invite us to reflect on the resilience and sustainability of our cities.

The "Burning City" and the "Great Flood"

One of Nostradamus's most chilling prophecies is found in Century I, Quatrain 87:

"The great city will be thoroughly burned,

The fire from the sky will cause it to fall,

The proud ones will be humbled."

This quatrain, with its vivid imagery of destruction, has been interpreted as a prediction of a major fire or bombardment destroying a prominent city. Some have linked it to historical events like the Great Fire of London in 1666 or the bombing of Hiroshima and Nagasaki in 1945.

Another quatrain that has fuelled speculation about urban disasters is Century I, Quatrain 69:

"The dry earth will grow more parched, and there will be great floods when it is seen."

This quatrain, with its stark contrast between drought and deluge, could be seen as a warning of extreme weather events affecting urban areas. Rising sea levels, intensified storms, and flash floods could all pose significant threats to coastal cities and low-lying areas.

Urban Development and the Rise of Smart Cities

While Nostradamus's prophecies paint a dire picture of potential urban disasters, they also hint at the potential for resilience and adaptation. In Century III, Quatrain 97, he speaks of a "new order of the centuries" that will bring about "great inventions" and "strange enterprises." This could be interpreted as a reference to the rise of smart cities, where technology is used to improve infrastructure, resource management, and disaster response.

The concept of smart cities has gained traction in recent years as urban planners and policymakers seek to address the challenges of urbanization, climate change, and resource scarcity. By integrating data and technology into urban planning and management, smart cities aim to create more sustainable, resilient, and liveable environments.

Nostradamus's prophecies, while not explicitly mentioning smart cities, could be seen as foreshadowing this trend towards technological innovation in urban development. The "great inventions" and "strange enterprises" mentioned in his verses could refer to the deployment of sensors, artificial intelligence, and other technologies to optimize energy use, traffic flow, and public safety.

The Future of Cities: A Nostradamian Perspective

Nostradamus's prophecies about cities, like all prophecies, are open to interpretation and debate. Skeptics argue that their apparent relevance to contemporary events is merely a result of confirmation bias and retrospective interpretation. However, even if we approach these prophecies with a healthy dose of scepticism, they still offer valuable food for thought.

As we face the challenges of the 21st century, Nostradamus's prophecies remind us of the inherent vulnerabilities of urban centres. They challenge us to consider the potential impact of natural disasters, climate change, and technological disruptions on our cities and to invest in measures to mitigate these risks.

At the same time, Nostradamus's verses also offer a glimmer of hope, suggesting that human ingenuity and technological innovation can play a role in creating more resilient and sustainable urban environments. By embracing a proactive and forward-thinking approach to urban planning and management, we can strive to build cities that are not only prepared for the challenges of the future but also capable of thriving in a changing world.

CHAPTER 16: COMMUNICATION EVOLUTION: BEYOND THE INTERNET

In our hyper-connected world, communication technologies have transformed the way we interact, learn, and perceive reality. Nostradamus, with his cryptic verses penned centuries before the advent of the internet, may have foreseen a future where communication transcends the boundaries of our current understanding. His prophecies, while shrouded in symbolism, offer a glimpse into potential breakthroughs in communication and their profound impact on society and human interaction.

The "Great Chatter" and the "Universal Language"

Nostradamus, in Century I, Quatrain 67, speaks of a time when "the great chatter will arise." This phrase has been interpreted by some as a prediction of the rise of social media and the global exchange of information facilitated by the internet. However, others believe it could allude to a more profound shift in communication, perhaps the development of a universal language or a new form of telepathic communication.

Century X, Quatrain 74, further fuels speculation about communication breakthroughs:

"The new law will occupy the new land,

Towards Syria, Judea, and Palestine:
The great barbarian empire will decay,
Before the Moon completes its cycle."
This quatrain speaks of a "new law" and a "new land," which some interpret as representing a new paradigm of communication that transcends geographical and cultural barriers. The decay of the "great barbarian empire" could be seen as a metaphor for the obsolescence of traditional communication methods in the face of this new paradigm.

The Advent of Brain-Computer Interfaces

In recent years, researchers have made significant progress in developing brain-computer interfaces (BCIs), which allow for direct communication between the brain and external devices. While still in their early stages, BCIs hold the potential to revolutionize communication for people with disabilities, enable new forms of creative expression, and even enhance our cognitive abilities.

Nostradamus, in Century III, Quatrain 34, speaks of a time when "the mind will be opened to the heavens." This could be interpreted as a prediction of the development of BCIs, which could enable us to communicate directly with our minds, bypassing the limitations of language and physical barriers.

The Impact on Society and Interpersonal Relationships

The potential impact of such communication breakthroughs is immense. A universal language could foster greater understanding and cooperation between cultures, while telepathic communication could revolutionize the way we interact with each other and the world around us.

However, these advancements also raise important ethical and social questions. How would telepathic communication affect our privacy and autonomy? Would a universal language homogenize cultures and erode diversity? How would BCIs impact our sense of self and identity?

Nostradamus's prophecies, with their cryptic warnings and enigmatic visions, challenge us to consider the potential consequences of our technological pursuits. They remind us that every breakthrough comes with its own set of challenges and that we must approach innovation with caution and foresight.

A Glimpse into the Future of Communication

As we stand on the cusp of a communication revolution, Nostradamus's prophecies offer a tantalizing glimpse into the possibilities that lie ahead. While his verses may not offer precise predictions, they inspire us to imagine a future where communication transcends the limitations of language and technology, where thoughts and ideas flow freely, and where the human mind is connected to the vast expanse of the universe.

As we explore this uncharted territory, it is crucial to engage in thoughtful and ethical discussions about the implications of these advancements. By balancing the pursuit of progress with a deep respect for human values, we can ensure that communication technologies serve to enrich our lives and connect us to each other in meaningful ways.

Questions for Reflection:

1. How do you interpret Nostradamus's prophecies about communication in the context of current technological advancements?

2. What are the potential benefits and risks of brain-computer interfaces and other emerging communication technologies?

3. How can we ensure that these technologies are developed and used in an ethical and responsible manner?

CHAPTER 17: WARFARE IN 2024: NEW FORMS OF CONFLICT

Nostradamus, a man who lived in an era of swords and shields, may seem an unlikely source for insights into the nature of 21st-century warfare. However, his enigmatic verses have been interpreted by some as containing eerily prescient glimpses into the changing landscape of conflict. As we grapple with the rise of cyberwarfare, the proliferation of advanced weaponry, and the blurring of lines between traditional and non-traditional battlegrounds, Nostradamus's prophecies offer a unique perspective on the evolving nature of war.

Visions of Fire and Fury

Nostradamus's quatrains are rife with imagery of conflict and destruction, with frequent references to "fire from the sky," "great battles," and "bloodshed." While these images could be interpreted as referring to traditional forms of warfare, some scholars suggest that they may also foreshadow new forms of conflict, such as cyberattacks and information warfare.

Century I, Quatrain 48, speaks of a "great plague" and "fire from the centre of the earth." This has been interpreted by some as a prediction of biological warfare or the use of nuclear weapons. While these interpretations may seem alarmist, they reflect the growing concerns about the potential for catastrophic consequences in modern warfare.

Century VIII, Quatrain 77, warns of a "great war" that will "last for seven months." This prediction has fuelled speculation about a prolonged global conflict, potentially involving multiple nations and spanning multiple domains.

The Rise of Cyberwarfare

In the digital age, cyberwarfare has emerged as a new and potent form of conflict. Cyberattacks can cripple critical infrastructure, disrupt economies, and sow chaos and confusion. The recent SolarWinds hack, in which Russian hackers infiltrated numerous U.S. government and private sector networks, serves as a stark reminder of the vulnerability of our digital systems.

Nostradamus, in Century IX, Quatrain 73, writes of a "new fire" that will "come from the depths of the earth." This could be interpreted as a reference to cyberattacks, which often originate from unknown sources and can have devastating consequences.

The Information Battlefield

In addition to cyberattacks, the 21st century has also witnessed the rise of information warfare, where disinformation, propaganda, and manipulation of public opinion are used as weapons. The spread of fake news and the use of social media to incite violence are just two examples of how information can be weaponized.

Nostradamus, in Century III, Quatrain 81, speaks of a time when "the written word will be so obfuscated, that no one will be able to understand it at all." This could be seen as a prediction of the proliferation of disinformation and the difficulty of discerning truth from falsehood in the digital age.

The Evolution of Military Technology

While Nostradamus's prophecies may not explicitly mention drones, hypersonic missiles, or other modern weapons, his references to "fire from the sky" and "machines that fly" could be interpreted as foreshadowing the development of advanced military technologies. The increasing use of autonomous weapons systems and the potential for AI-powered warfare raise profound ethical and strategic questions.

Nostradamus's prophecies, with their cryptic warnings and enigmatic visions, challenge us to consider the changing nature of warfare in the 21st century. They remind us that conflict is no longer confined to traditional battlefields and that new forms of warfare pose unique challenges and risks.

As we navigate this complex landscape, it is essential to prioritize diplomacy, cooperation, and international law. We must also invest in cybersecurity, information literacy, and the development of ethical guidelines for the use of emerging technologies. Only by working together can we ensure that the future of warfare is not one of destruction and chaos, but of peace and stability.

CHAPTER 18:
OCEANIC MYSTERIES UNVEILED

In the vast expanse of Nostradamus's prophetic verses, the world's oceans emerge as a recurring motif, shrouded in mystery and brimming with untapped potential. His quatrains, with their allusions to rising tides, hidden depths, and enigmatic creatures, have captivated the imaginations of interpreters for centuries. As we delve into these oceanic prophecies, we uncover a fascinating interplay between ancient wisdom and modern scientific discoveries, prompting us to reflect on the profound mysteries that lie beneath the waves.

The "Great Flood" and Rising Seas

Nostradamus, in Century I, Quatrain 69, writes:

"The dry earth will grow more parched, and there will be great floods when it is seen."

This quatrain, with its stark contrast between drought and deluge, has been interpreted by some as a warning of rising sea levels and the potential inundation of coastal cities. As climate change accelerates, this prophecy seems eerily prescient, with scientific models predicting significant sea-level rise by the end of the 21st century.

However, other interpreters suggest that this quatrain could be a metaphor for broader social and political upheaval, with the "great floods" representing a wave of change sweeping across the world. This interpretation aligns with Nostradamus's tendency to use natural imagery to symbolize human events and historical trends.

Uncharted Depths: The Search for Hidden Worlds

Nostradamus's quatrains also hint at the potential for ground-breaking discoveries in the depths of the ocean. Century II, Quatrain 29, speaks of "new lands" that will be discovered, which some interpret as a reference to underwater civilizations or previously unknown ecosystems.

In the 21st century, ocean exploration has revealed a wealth of biodiversity and geological wonders. The discovery of hydrothermal vents teeming with life and the mapping of vast underwater mountain ranges have challenged our understanding of the ocean's potential. As technology advances, we may yet uncover even more astonishing secrets hidden beneath the waves.

The Ocean's Influence on Global Climate

The ocean plays a crucial role in regulating Earth's climate, absorbing heat and carbon dioxide, and influencing weather patterns. Nostradamus's prophecies, with their references to extreme weather events and changing climates, could be seen as acknowledging the ocean's profound impact on our planet. Century VI, Quatrain 58, speaks of a time when "the great ocean will change its course." This could be interpreted as a warning of disruptions to ocean currents, such as the Gulf Stream, which could have far-reaching consequences for global weather patterns and ecosystems.

The Enigma of Nostradamus's Oceanic Prophecies

Nostradamus's prophecies about the ocean, like all his verses, are open to interpretation and debate. Some scholars, like Edgar Leoni, argue that his references to the ocean are primarily symbolic, representing the vastness and unpredictability of the human experience (Leoni, 1961). Others, like Dolores Cannon, believe that his prophecies contain specific warnings about environmental disasters and the need for humanity to protect the oceans (Cannon, 2002).

Regardless of interpretation, Nostradamus's prophecies serve as a reminder of the ocean's power and mystery. They challenge us to explore the depths of this vast and largely unknown realm, to unravel its secrets, and to understand its vital role in shaping our planet's future.

As we continue to explore the ocean's depths and grapple with the challenges of climate change, Nostradamus's prophecies serve as a timeless reminder of the interconnectedness of all life on Earth and the importance of safeguarding our planet's most precious resources.

CHAPTER 19: THE ROLE OF WOMEN IN 2024: RISING TO PROMINENCE

In the patriarchal world of 16th-century France, Nostradamus's cryptic verses occasionally touch upon the role of women in society. While his predictions are often veiled in symbolism and open to interpretation, some scholars believe they foreshadow a future where women rise to positions of power and influence, challenging traditional gender roles and reshaping the global landscape.

The "Great Lady" and the "Queen of the World"

One of Nostradamus's most intriguing prophecies concerning women is found in Century VI, Quatrain 77:

"A great lady from the East will come,

To reign in the new land of the Eagle,

She will defeat the old powers,

And bring about a new era of peace."

This quatrain has been interpreted in various ways, with some suggesting it refers to a female political leader from Asia who will rise to prominence on the world stage. The "new land of the Eagle" could be seen as a reference to the United States, while the "old powers" could represent traditional political establishments or patriarchal structures.

Another quatrain that has fuelled speculation about female

leadership is Century III, Quatrain 62:
"A queen will come from the East,
Who will enchant the world with her beauty and wisdom,
She will unite nations and bring harmony,
But her reign will be short-lived."

This quatrain paints a picture of a charismatic female leader who will inspire global unity and cooperation. However, the prophecy also hints at the challenges and limitations of female leadership in a world still grappling with gender inequality.

The Rise of Female Leaders in 2024

As of 2024, women have made significant strides in political leadership across the globe. In recent years, we have witnessed the election of several female heads of state and government, including Jacinda Ardern in New Zealand, Sanna Marin in Finland, and Kamala Harris in the United States as Vice President.

While Nostradamus's prophecies do not explicitly mention these specific leaders, their rise to power could be seen as a partial fulfilment of his predictions. The growing representation of women in politics is a testament to the ongoing struggle for gender equality and the evolving role of women in society.

Challenges and Opportunities for Women in 2024

Despite the progress made in recent years, women still face significant barriers to leadership in many parts of the world. Gender discrimination, societal expectations, and structural inequalities continue to hinder women's advancement in various fields.

Nostradamus's prophecies, with their warnings of conflict and upheaval, may also foreshadow challenges and setbacks for women in 2024. The quatrain Century VIII, Quatrain 77, speaks of "great troubles" and "persecutions" that could be interpreted as a reference to the backlash against women's empowerment and the ongoing struggle for gender equality.

However, Nostradamus's prophecies also offer a message of hope. The "great lady" and the "queen of the world" mentioned in his verses could represent the potential for women to overcome these challenges and to lead the world towards a more just and equitable future.

The Future of Gender Equality: A Nostradamian Perspective

Nostradamus's prophecies, while open to interpretation, provide a unique lens through which to view the evolving role of women in society. They challenge us to consider the potential for female leadership to transform the world and to address the systemic inequalities that hinder women's progress.

As we navigate the complexities of the 21st century, Nostradamus's prophecies remind us that the future is not predetermined. The choices we make today will shape the world of tomorrow. By embracing gender equality and empowering women in all spheres of life, we can create a future where the prophecies of female leadership become a reality, not just a cryptic verse from the past.

CHAPTER 20: GENETIC ENGINEERING: REWRITING HUMAN DNA

Nostradamus, a visionary seer of the 16th century, lived in a world where the secrets of DNA and genetics were yet to be unlocked. However, some interpretations of his quatrains suggest that he may have glimpsed a future where humanity wields the power to manipulate the very code of life itself. As we stand on the precipice of a genetic revolution, with CRISPR-Cas9 and other gene-editing technologies reshaping our understanding of human potential, Nostradamus's cryptic verses offer a unique perspective on the ethical dilemmas and transformative possibilities of this scientific frontier.

The "Hidden Arts" and the "New Man"

In Century I, Quatrain 63, Nostradamus writes:

_"The hidden arts will come to light,

The world will be renewed by a new man,

Who will know the secrets of the stars,

And will change the course of human destiny."_

Some interpreters believe that the "hidden arts" refer to genetic engineering, a field that was unknown in Nostradamus's time but has emerged as a powerful tool for manipulating the genetic code of living organisms. The "new man" could represent a future generation of humans who have been genetically modified to possess enhanced traits or to be resistant to diseases.

Another quatrain that has been linked to genetic engineering is Century IX, Quatrain 44:

_"From the sky will come a great King of Terror,

To bring back to life the great King of Angoumois,

Before after Mars to reign by good luck."_

This quatrain speaks of a "great King of Terror" who will "bring back to life" another king. Some interpret this as a prediction of the resurrection of extinct species or the creation of genetically engineered organisms with unprecedented capabilities.

The Ethical Dilemmas of Human Enhancement

The prospect of genetic engineering raises profound ethical questions about the limits of human intervention in the natural world. Should we use gene-editing technologies to enhance human traits, such as intelligence, athletic ability, or longevity? What are the potential consequences of creating designer babies or a genetic elite?

Nostradamus's prophecies, with their warnings of "great misfortunes" and "terrible events," could be interpreted as cautionary tales about the potential dangers of unchecked genetic manipulation. The "new man" mentioned in Century I, Quatrain 63, could represent a dystopian future where humanity has lost touch with its natural origins and has become enslaved to its own technological creations.

The Promise of Genetic Cures

While the potential for human enhancement is fraught with ethical concerns, genetic engineering also holds the promise of curing genetic diseases and improving human health. CRISPR-Cas9, a revolutionary gene-editing tool, has already shown promise in treating sickle cell anaemia, cystic fibrosis, and other genetic disorders.

Nostradamus's prophecies, while often focused on doom and

gloom, also offer glimpses of hope. Century X, Quatrain 74,speaks of a "great discovery" that will "renew the age." This could be interpreted as a reference to breakthroughs in genetic medicine that will eradicate diseases and extend human lifespans.

The Genetic Revolution: A Nostradamian Perspective

Nostradamus's prophecies, while open to interpretation, offer a unique and thought-provoking perspective on the ethical dilemmas and transformative possibilities of genetic engineering. As we venture into this uncharted territory, we must proceed with caution, guided by a deep respect for human dignity and the sanctity of life.

The decisions we make today will shape the future of our species. By embracing a responsible and ethical approach to genetic engineering, we can harness the power of this technology to alleviate suffering, enhance human potential, and create a healthier and more equitable world for all.

CHAPTER 21: THE TRANSFORMATION OF EDUCATION

In the realm of Nostradamus' prophecies, the future of education emerges as a fascinating and multifaceted tapestry. His enigmatic verses, woven with threads of symbolism and allegory, hint at both the disruption of traditional educational systems and the emergence of new paradigms of learning. As we navigate the complexities of the 21st century, these prophecies offer a unique perspective on the challenges and opportunities that lie ahead for education.

The "Hidden Knowledge" and the "New Sages"

Nostradamus, in Century III, Quatrain 97, speaks of a time when "the hidden knowledge will be revealed." This enigmatic phrase has been interpreted in various ways, with some suggesting it refers to the democratization of knowledge through the internet and digital technologies. Others believe it alludes to the discovery of new scientific or philosophical truths that will revolutionize our understanding of the world.

In Century I, Quatrain 48, Nostradamus mentions "new sages" who will "guide the world towards enlightenment." This could be interpreted as a prediction of the rise of new educators, thought leaders, and influencers who will challenge traditional educational norms and inspire new ways of thinking and learning.

The Rise of EdTech and Online Learning

In recent years, educational technology (EdTech) has transformed the landscape of learning, with online courses, virtual classrooms, and adaptive learning platforms becoming increasingly prevalent. The COVID-19 pandemic further accelerated this trend, as schools and universities around the world were forced to embrace remote learning.

Nostradamus's prophecies, while not explicitly mentioning EdTech, could be seen as foreshadowing this shift towards digital education. Century X, Quatrain 72, speaks of a "new way of teaching" that will "spread throughout the world." This could be interpreted as a reference to the global reach and accessibility of online learning platforms.

The Emergence of New Fields of Study

As the world becomes more complex and interconnected, the need for interdisciplinary knowledge and skills is growing. Nostradamus's prophecies, with their focus on the intersection of science, spirituality, and philosophy, could be seen as foreshadowing the emergence of new fields of study that transcend traditional disciplinary boundaries.

Century VI, Quatrain 62, speaks of a time when "the secrets of nature will be revealed." This could be interpreted as a prediction of breakthroughs in fields like biotechnology, nanotechnology, and artificial intelligence, which are already blurring the lines between different scientific disciplines.

The Challenges and Opportunities of Educational Transformation

The transformation of education, while offering immense potential for innovation and progress, also poses significant challenges. The rapid pace of technological change requires educators and institutions to adapt quickly and embrace new pedagogical approaches. The widening digital divide threatens to exacerbate existing educational inequalities, with marginalized communities at risk of being left behind.

Nostradamus's prophecies, with their warnings of "great changes" and "unexpected events," serve as a reminder of the need for flexibility and resilience in the face of educational disruption. They also challenge us to consider the ethical implications of emerging technologies and to ensure that education remains a force for social good.

A Nostradamian Vision for the Future of Education

Nostradamus's prophecies, while open to interpretation, offer a unique and thought-provoking perspective on the evolving landscape of education. They challenge us to envision a future where learning is not confined to traditional classrooms, where knowledge is accessible to all, and where new fields of study emerge to address the complex challenges of our time.

By embracing innovation, collaboration, and a lifelong love of learning, we can create a future where education empowers individuals, strengthens communities, and fosters a more just and sustainable world.

CHAPTER 22: THE FUTURE OF WORK: AUTOMATION AND BEYOND

In the age of artificial intelligence, robotics, and automation, Nostradamus's prophecies find a curious resonance. His quatrains, penned in the 16th century, offer glimpses into a future where work and livelihood undergo profound transformations. While these verses are laden with symbolism and open to interpretation, they prompt us to contemplate the potential impact of technological advancements on the job market, the rise of new professions, and the societal implications of a changing economic landscape.

The "Great Unemployment" and the "New Masters"

Nostradamus, in Century I, Quatrain 87, speaks of a "new engine" that will cause "great riches to change masters." This enigmatic verse has been interpreted by some as a foreshadowing of the rise of automation and its potential to displace workers and disrupt traditional industries.

In the 21st century, we are already witnessing the impact of automation on the job market, with robots and algorithms replacing humans in manufacturing, transportation, and customer service. The fear of a "great unemployment," where millions of jobs become obsolete, looms large in the minds of many.

However, other interpretations of Nostradamus's prophecy offer a more nuanced perspective. The "new engine" could also represent a technological breakthrough that creates new industries and job opportunities. For instance, the rise of artificial intelligence has led to the emergence of new professions in fields such as data science, machine learning, and robotics.

The Rise of New Professions and the Obsolescence of Others

Nostradamus's quatrains also hint at the rise and fall of different professions. In Century III, Quatrain 54, he writes of a time when "the great ones will be humbled" and "the humble will be exalted." This could be interpreted as a prediction of the decline of traditional white-collar jobs and the rise of new professions that require different skills and expertise.

The advent of the gig economy, the increasing demand for digital skills, and the growing importance of creativity and emotional intelligence are already transforming the workplace. Nostradamus's prophecies, while vague and open to interpretation, could be seen as reflecting these ongoing changes.

Universal Basic Income: A Nostradamian Solution?

As automation continues to displace workers, some have proposed the idea of a universal basic income (UBI) as a way to provide financial security for those whose jobs have been automated. UBI is a form of social security in which all citizens or residents of a country receive a regular, unconditional sum of money, regardless of their income or employment status.

Nostradamus, in Century II, Quatrain 46, speaks of a time when "the great cycle of the centuries renewed, it will rain blood, milk, famine, war and disease." This quatrain paints a bleak picture of social and economic upheaval. However, some interpreters see the reference to "milk" as a symbolic representation of a basic sustenance provided to all, which could be seen as a foreshadowing of UBI.

The Future of Work: A Nostradamian Perspective

Nostradamus's prophecies, while not offering concrete

predictions about the future of work, provide a thought-provoking framework for contemplating the potential impact of technological advancements on our livelihoods. They challenge us to think critically about the changing nature of work, the skills that will be in demand in the future, and the policies we need to implement to ensure that everyone has the opportunity to thrive in a rapidly changing economy.

As we navigate the uncertainties of the 21st century, Nostradamus's prophecies remind us that change is inevitable. By embracing innovation, adapting to new technologies, and investing in education and skills training, we can create a future of work that is both prosperous and equitable.

Questions for Reflection:

1.	How do you interpret Nostradamus's prophecies about the future of work in the context of current technological advancements?

2.	What new professions do you think will emerge in the coming years, and which ones are most likely to become obsolete?

3.	Do you believe that universal basic income is a viable solution to the challenges posed by automation?

CHAPTER 23: VIRTUAL REALITIES: THE NEW FRONTIER

The concept of alternate realities, once confined to the realm of science fiction and fantasy, is inching closer to reality. Advancements in virtual reality (VR) and augmented reality (AR) technologies are blurring the lines between the physical and digital worlds, creating immersive experiences that challenge our perceptions of what is real and what is possible. In the prophetic verses of Nostradamus, we find intriguing hints of this emerging reality, prompting us to reflect on the societal implications of widespread VR adoption.

The "Mirror of the World"

In Century III, Quatrain 94, Nostradamus writes:

"In the city of God there will be a great thunder,

Two brothers torn apart by chaos,

While the fortress endures, the great leader will succumb,

The third big war will begin when the big city is burning."

While this quatrain is often interpreted as a prediction of war and destruction, some scholars suggest that it could also be seen as a metaphor for the blurring of boundaries between the real world and virtual realms. The "great thunder" could represent the disruptive impact of VR technology, while the "two brothers torn apart by chaos" could symbolize the fragmentation of identity and reality that can occur in virtual environments.

The "New World" of Virtual Experiences

In Century X, Quatrain 74, Nostradamus speaks of a "new law" that will "occupy the new land." This has been interpreted by some as a prediction of the rise of virtual worlds and their potential to reshape our social, economic, and cultural landscapes.

In recent years, we have witnessed the emergence of immersive virtual platforms like Meta's Horizon Worlds and Decentraland, where users can interact with each other, create digital assets, and even own virtual real estate. These virtual worlds are still in their early stages, but they offer a glimpse into a future where we may spend significant amounts of time in alternate realities.

The Potential and Perils of VR Adoption

The widespread adoption of VR technology has the potential to revolutionize numerous fields, from education and healthcare to entertainment and communication. For example, VR could enable immersive learning experiences, provide therapy for mental health conditions, and create new forms of social interaction.

However, as Nostradamus's prophecies suggest, this new frontier also comes with potential risks and challenges. The blurring of boundaries between the real and virtual worlds could lead to addiction, social isolation, and a loss of connection to physical reality. There are also concerns about the potential for VR to be used for manipulation, propaganda, and other nefarious purposes.

The Nostradamian Lens on Virtual Realities

Nostradamus's prophecies, while open to interpretation, offer a valuable framework for contemplating the societal implications of VR. They encourage us to consider the potential benefits and risks of this technology, and to approach its development and adoption with caution and foresight.

As we venture into this new frontier, it is crucial to prioritize ethical considerations and ensure that VR technologies are designed and used in ways that promote human well-being and social cohesion. This involves fostering a multi-stakeholder dialogue that includes technologists, policymakers, educators, and the public to ensure that the development of VR is guided by ethical principles and societal needs.

By embracing a thoughtful and responsible approach to VR, we can harness its transformative power to enhance our lives, expand our horizons, and create new forms of connection and understanding.

Questions for Reflection:

1.	How do you interpret Nostradamus's prophecies about virtual realities in the context of current technological developments?

2.	What are the potential benefits and risks of widespread VR adoption?

3.	How can we ensure that VR technologies are developed and used in an ethical and responsible manner?

CHAPTER 24:
THE EVOLUTION
OF HUMAN
RELATIONSHIPS

Nostradamus's cryptic quatrains, while often focused on grand events and historical figures, also offer intriguing glimpses into the future of human relationships. As society grapples with shifting demographics, technological advancements, and changing cultural norms, Nostradamus's prophecies raise questions about the evolution of family structures, romantic partnerships, and social connections in the 21st century.

Love and Loss in the Age of Aquarius

Century III, Quatrain 35, speaks of a time when "the great cycle of the centuries renewed, it will rain blood, milk, famine, war and disease." This apocalyptic vision, often interpreted as a prediction of global upheaval, can also be seen as a metaphor for the turbulence and uncertainty that can characterize human relationships.

In Century II, Quatrain 61, Nostradamus writes:

_The two will not remain united for very long,
And in thirteen years to the Barbarian Satrap:
On both sides they will cause such loss,
That one will bless the bark and its cope._

This quatrain has been interpreted as a prediction of a short-lived alliance or partnership that will ultimately lead to conflict and loss. Some scholars believe it could refer to a political alliance, while others see it as a commentary on the fleeting nature of romantic relationships.

The Digital Age: Connecting and Disconnecting

In the 21st century, technology has revolutionized the way we connect with each other. Social media platforms, dating apps, and video conferencing tools have enabled us to form relationships across vast distances and maintain connections with loved ones in real-time.

However, Nostradamus's prophecies also warn of the potential for technology to isolate and disconnect us from each other. In Century I, Quatrain 55, he writes:

_The great famine will return, and then it will be all over the world,
So great and long that they will grab roots from the trees,
And children from the breast._

This quatrain, while often interpreted as a prediction of widespread famine, could also be seen as a metaphor for the emotional and spiritual hunger that can arise from a lack of genuine human connection. In a world where virtual interactions increasingly replace face-to-face encounters, the risk of social isolation and loneliness looms large.

Shifting Social Norms and Values

Nostradamus's prophecies also hint at changing social norms and values surrounding marriage, family, and gender roles. Century I, Quatrain 28, speaks of a time when "marriage will be celebrated without the priests." This could be interpreted as a prediction of the rise of secularism and the decline of traditional religious institutions, or it could foreshadow a future where marriage is redefined to include same-sex couples or other non-traditional arrangements.

Century IX, Quatrain 47, mentions a "great change" in the "rule of women." This could be interpreted as a prediction of the growing empowerment of women and their increasing participation in all spheres of life, including politics, business, and the arts.

The Future of Human Relationships: A Nostradamian Perspective

Nostradamus's prophecies, while open to interpretation, offer a unique lens through which to view the evolving landscape of human relationships. They challenge us to consider the impact of technology, changing social norms, and global events on our connections with each other.

While some of his predictions may seem bleak, they also offer a message of hope and resilience. The human spirit, as Nostradamus suggests, is capable of adapting to change and finding new ways to connect and thrive. By embracing empathy, communication, and a willingness to evolve, we can create a future where relationships are strengthened, not weakened, by the challenges and opportunities of the 21st century.

As we navigate the uncharted waters of the future, Nostradamus's prophecies serve as a reminder of the enduring power of human connection. Whether his verses are seen as literal predictions or metaphorical musings, they invite us to reflect on the importance of love, compassion, and community in our lives.

CHAPTER 25: THE GREAT AWAKENING: A CONSCIOUSNESS SHIFT?

As 2024 unfolds, a recurring theme in discussions surrounding Nostradamus's prophecies is the potential for a significant shift in human consciousness. While the concept of a "Great Awakening" is not explicitly mentioned in his quatrains, numerous verses hint at spiritual transformation, the questioning of established norms, and the emergence of new philosophical movements.

Nostradamus, a man steeped in Renaissance esotericism and Hermetic philosophy, believed in the interconnectedness of all things and the cyclical nature of history. His prophecies, while often focused on specific events, can also be seen as reflections on broader spiritual and philosophical themes.

The "Hidden Knowledge" and the "New Sages"

In Century III, Quatrain 97, Nostradamus speaks of a time when "the hidden knowledge will be revealed." This enigmatic phrase has been interpreted in various ways, with some suggesting it refers to the democratization of knowledge through the internet and digital technologies, while others believe it alludes to the rediscovery of ancient wisdom and spiritual practices.

In the context of a potential "Great Awakening," this

quatrain could be seen as a foreshadowing of a global shift in consciousness, where people seek deeper meaning and connection beyond the material world. This could manifest as a renewed interest in spirituality, meditation, mindfulness, or other practices that foster self-awareness and inner peace.

Century I, Quatrain 48, mentions "new sages" who will "guide the world towards enlightenment." This could be interpreted as a prediction of the emergence of new spiritual leaders, thought leaders, or influencers who will challenge conventional thinking and inspire a new wave of consciousness.

In a world grappling with existential threats like climate change, political polarization, and social unrest, the yearning for meaning and purpose is palpable. Nostradamus's prophecies, with their emphasis on spiritual transformation and the search for truth, resonate with this deep-seated human need.

The Role of Ancient Wisdom in Modern Times

Nostradamus himself was deeply influenced by ancient wisdom traditions, drawing on astrology, kabbalah, and Hermetic philosophy to inform his prophecies. In the 21st century, there is a growing interest in these ancient practices, as people seek alternative ways of understanding the world and their place within it.

The resurgence of interest in astrology, for example, can be seen as a manifestation of this yearning for deeper meaning and connection to the cosmos. The popularity of mindfulness and meditation practices also reflects a growing desire for inner peace and self-awareness.

Nostradamus's prophecies, while not explicitly endorsing any particular spiritual practice, suggest that ancient wisdom has a vital role to play in navigating the challenges of the modern world. By drawing on the insights of past generations, we can gain a broader perspective on our current predicament and find new ways to address the complex issues facing humanity.

A Skeptical Perspective

While some interpret Nostradamus's prophecies as evidence of a potential "Great Awakening," others remain skeptical. They argue that his verses are too vague and open to interpretation to be considered reliable predictions of future events. Skeptics also caution against reading too much into the current interest in spirituality and ancient wisdom, suggesting that it may be a passing trend rather than a lasting shift in consciousness.

The Future of Consciousness: A Nostradamian Reflection

Whether or not Nostradamus accurately predicted a "Great Awakening," his prophecies offer a valuable opportunity for reflection and introspection. They invite us to consider the deeper meaning and purpose of our lives, to explore the potential of human consciousness, and to seek connection with something greater than ourselves.

As we navigate the uncertainties of the 21st century, Nostradamus's prophecies serve as a reminder of the timeless wisdom that can be found in ancient traditions. By embracing open-mindedness, curiosity, and a willingness to learn from the past, we can cultivate a more enlightened and compassionate future for ourselves and for generations to come.

CHAPTER 26: TRANSPORTATION REVOLUTION: FROM NOSTRADAMUS TO NOW

In the heart of the 16th century, Nostradamus penned cryptic verses that have intrigued and perplexed scholars for centuries. While his prophecies often centre on political intrigue and social upheaval, some quatrains offer tantalizing glimpses into the future of transportation. As we navigate a world of electric vehicles, autonomous drones, and burgeoning hyperloop projects, these prophecies prompt us to reflect on the transformative power of technological innovation and the potential for radical shifts in how we traverse the globe.

The "Iron Bird" Takes Flight

Nostradamus, in Century IX, Quatrain 41, writes of "iron birds" that will "traverse the sky." This evocative image has been interpreted by some as a prediction of the advent of airplanes, a mode of transportation that was unimaginable in Nostradamus's time.

In the 21st century, air travel has become ubiquitous, connecting people and cultures across vast distances. The rise of commercial aviation has revolutionized global trade, tourism, and communication. However, the environmental impact of air travel has raised concerns about its sustainability.

Nostradamus's prophecy, while potentially referring to the invention of airplanes, could also be seen as a broader commentary on the human desire to conquer the skies and the challenges that come with it.

Electric Dreams and Autonomous Visions

In recent years, electric vehicles (EVs) have emerged as a viable alternative to gasoline-powered cars. The growing popularity of EVs is driven by concerns about climate change, air pollution, and the desire for more sustainable transportation options.

Nostradamus, in Century II, Quatrain 46, speaks of a time when "the great cycle of the centuries renewed, it will rain blood, milk, famine, war and disease." While this quatrain is often interpreted as a prediction of global upheaval, some scholars suggest that the reference to "milk" could be seen as a symbol of clean energy, such as electricity generated from renewable sources.

Furthermore, the rise of autonomous vehicles (AVs) promises to revolutionize transportation by reducing accidents, improving traffic flow, and enhancing accessibility. Nostradamus's prophecies, while not explicitly mentioning AVs, could be interpreted as foreshadowing a future where machines play a more significant role in transportation.

Hyperloop: A Nostradamian Dream?

The concept of a hyperloop, a high-speed transportation system that propels pods through low-pressure tubes, has captured the imagination of innovators and futurists. This revolutionary technology has the potential to drastically reduce travel times and energy consumption.

Nostradamus, in Century IV, Quatrain 35, writes of a "great tunnel" that will "connect two seas." This could be seen as a reference to a hyperloop system that spans vast distances, connecting cities and continents in a matter of hours.

While hyperloop technology is still in its early stages of development, several projects are underway around the world, including Virgin Hyperloop and the Boring Company's Loop. These projects could potentially transform the way we travel and commute, making long-distance travel faster, more efficient, and more accessible.

The Road Ahead: A Nostradamian Perspective

Nostradamus's prophecies, while open to interpretation, offer a unique perspective on the future of transportation. They challenge us to envision a world where technological innovation redefines how we move and connect with each other.

As we embrace electric vehicles, autonomous vehicles, and potentially even hyperloop technology, we must also consider the ethical, social, and environmental implications of these advancements. How will these technologies impact employment, urban planning, and social interactions? How can we ensure that they are accessible and equitable for all?

Nostradamus's prophecies serve as a reminder that the future of transportation is not predetermined. Our choices and actions today will shape the world of tomorrow. By embracing innovation, sustainability, and a commitment to social responsibility, we can create a transportation system that is both efficient and equitable, serving the needs of both people and the planet.

CHAPTER 27: THE FATE OF WORLD RELIGIONS: SHIFTING SANDS OF FAITH

In Nostradamus's prophetic landscape, religion and spirituality play a prominent role. His quatrains, steeped in biblical imagery and astrological symbolism, have been interpreted as foretelling both the decline of established faiths and the emergence of new spiritual movements. As we navigate an increasingly interconnected and diverse world, these prophecies invite us to reflect on the evolving nature of belief systems and the potential for both conflict and unity among different faiths.

The "Great Heresy" and the "New Law"

One of Nostradamus's most debated prophecies concerning religion is found in Century X, Quatrain 75:

_"Long awaited, he will never return

In Europe, he will appear in Asia:

One of the league issued from the great Hermes,

And he will grow over all the Kings of the East."_

This quatrain has been interpreted in various ways, with some suggesting it refers to the emergence of a new religious figure or a radical reinterpretation of existing faiths. The reference to "Hermes," the Greek god of messengers and tricksters, could symbolize a figure who challenges traditional beliefs and disrupts established power structures.

In Century II, Quatrain 29, Nostradamus speaks of a "new law" that will "occupy the great world." This could be interpreted as a prediction of the rise of a new global religion or a major shift in religious consciousness. It could also refer to the growing influence of secularism and the decline of traditional religious authority.

The Rise and Fall of Religious Institutions

Nostradamus's prophecies also touch upon the fate of established religious institutions. Century VIII, Quatrain 96, warns of a time when "the clergy will be greatly weakened" and "the temples will be plundered." This could be seen as a prediction of the declining influence of organized religion in the face of secularization, scientific advancements, and the rise of alternative spiritual practices.

However, Nostradamus also hints at the potential for religious revival and renewal. Century I, Quatrain 50, speaks of a "new sect" that will "bring about great changes." This could be interpreted as a reference to a new religious movement that challenges the status quo and inspires a spiritual awakening.

Conflict and Cooperation Between Faiths

Throughout history, religion has been a source of both conflict and cooperation. Nostradamus's prophecies reflect this duality, with some quatrains warning of religious wars and persecution, while others speak of interfaith dialogue and collaboration.

Century III, Quatrain 97, speaks of a time when "the two religions will make war against each other." This could be seen as a prediction of escalating tensions between different faiths, or a broader commentary on the dangers of religious extremism and intolerance.

However, other quatrains offer a more hopeful vision. Century VI, Quatrain 21, speaks of a "great peace" that will be achieved through the "union of religions." This could be interpreted as a prediction of increased interfaith dialogue and cooperation, leading to a more harmonious and tolerant world.

The Nostradamian Lens on Religion in 2024

As we navigate the complexities of the 21st century, Nostradamus's prophecies offer a unique perspective on the evolving landscape of religion and spirituality. They challenge us to consider the potential for both conflict and cooperation between faiths, the decline of traditional institutions, and the emergence of new spiritual movements.

While Nostradamus's verses are open to interpretation, they serve as a reminder of the enduring power of faith and the importance of seeking meaning and purpose in our lives. Whether we choose to embrace traditional religions, explore alternative spiritual paths, or reject organized religion altogether, the quest for spiritual fulfilment remains a fundamental aspect of the human experience.

As we ponder the fate of world religions in 2024 and beyond, Nostradamus's prophecies invite us to engage in open-minded dialogue, to respect diverse beliefs, and to strive for a world where faith is a source of unity, not division.

CHAPTER 28: BIOENGINEERING: MERGING MAN AND MACHINE

The advent of the 21st century has ushered in an era of unprecedented advancements in biotechnology and genetic engineering, blurring the lines between the natural and the artificial. As we delve into Nostradamus's enigmatic quatrains, we find intriguing allusions to a future where humans merge with machines, enhancing their capabilities and transcending biological limitations. While these prophecies are open to interpretation, they prompt us to confront the ethical implications and societal ramifications of bioengineering and the potential emergence of transhumanism.

The "Iron Man" and the "New Creature"

In Century I, Quatrain 87, Nostradamus writes:

_The new engine will cause great riches to change masters,
Raised to heights, the bold one will be lowered by fortune._

This quatrain has been interpreted by some as a foreshadowing of the rise of robotics and artificial intelligence, but others see it as a reference to the integration of technology into the human body. The "new engine" could symbolize a revolutionary advancement in bioengineering, such as bionic limbs or neural implants, that enhances human capabilities and alters the balance of power.

In Century II, Quatrain 41, Nostradamus speaks of a "new creature" that will emerge from the earth, causing "great terror and confusion." This could be interpreted as a prediction of genetically modified organisms or even the creation of human-machine hybrids, blurring the lines between the natural and the artificial.

The Rise of Bionics and Neural Implants

In recent years, we have witnessed significant advancements in bionics and neural implants. Prosthetic limbs controlled by the brain, cochlear implants that restore hearing, and deep brain stimulation for Parkinson's disease are just a few examples of how technology is already augmenting human capabilities.

Nostradamus's prophecies, while written centuries ago, seem to echo these developments, hinting at a future where the integration of man and machine becomes commonplace. The ethical implications of such advancements are profound, raising questions about what it means to be human, the potential for creating a divide between the enhanced and the unenhanced, and the potential for misuse of these technologies.

The Transhumanist Vision

The concept of transhumanism, the belief that humans can transcend their biological limitations through technology, has gained traction in recent years. Proponents of transhumanism envision a future where humans can enhance their physical and cognitive abilities, live longer and healthier lives, and even achieve immortality.

Nostradamus's prophecies, with their references to "immortal" beings and "new creatures," could be seen as early glimpses of this transhumanist vision. However, the potential consequences of such radical transformations remain a subject of intense debate.

The Ethical Challenges of Bioengineering

The rapid advancement of bioengineering raises complex ethical questions about the limits of human intervention in the natural world. Should we allow genetic modifications that enhance human traits, such as intelligence or athleticism? Should we create artificial life forms or merge humans with machines?

Nostradamus's prophecies, with their warnings of "great terror and confusion," serve as a reminder of the potential dangers of unchecked technological progress. As we explore the possibilities of bioengineering, it is crucial to engage in open and transparent discussions about the ethical implications of these technologies and to develop robust governance frameworks to ensure their responsible use.

A Nostradamian Perspective on Bioengineering

Nostradamus's prophecies, while open to interpretation, offer a unique and thought-provoking lens through which to view the future of bioengineering. They challenge us to confront the ethical dilemmas of human enhancement, to consider the potential consequences of merging man and machine, and to envision a future where technology is used to enhance human potential without sacrificing our humanity.

As we navigate the uncharted waters of the 21st century, Nostradamus's prophecies serve as a reminder of the importance of foresight, ethical responsibility, and a commitment to the common good. By embracing a balanced and thoughtful approach to bioengineering, we can strive to create a future where technology enhances our lives, expands our capabilities, and upholds our shared values.

CHAPTER 29: THE NEW SPACE RACE: NOSTRADAMUS'S COSMIC PREDICTIONS REVISITED

As humanity ventures further into the cosmos, the echoes of Nostradamus's cryptic prophecies resonate with newfound relevance. While his verses were written in the 16th century, long before the advent of space exploration, some interpreters believe they contain tantalizing hints about a new space race, the colonization of other celestial bodies, and the potential for ground-breaking discoveries beyond our planet.

The "Iron Bird" Takes Flight, Again

Nostradamus, in Century IX, Quatrain 41, speaks of "iron birds" that will "traverse the sky." While this prophecy has often been linked to the invention of airplanes, it could also be interpreted as foreshadowing the modern era of spaceflight, with rockets and spacecraft replacing the feathered creatures of the past.

In 2024, we are witnessing a resurgence of interest in space exploration, driven not only by government agencies like

NASA and ESA but also by private companies like SpaceX, Blue Origin, and Virgin Galactic. These companies are competing to develop reusable spacecraft, launch satellites, and even establish permanent settlements on the Moon and Mars.

This new space race, fuelled by technological innovation and commercial interests, could be seen as a fulfilment of Nostradamus's prophecy. The "iron birds" are no longer mere symbols of human ingenuity; they are tangible vehicles that carry our aspirations and ambitions beyond the confines of Earth.

Colonizing the "New Land": The Moon and Mars

Nostradamus, in Century II, Quatrain 29, speaks of "new lands" that will be discovered. While this quatrain could be interpreted in various ways, some see it as a prediction of the colonization of the Moon or Mars, both of which have been identified as potential sites for human settlements.

In recent years, there has been a renewed focus on lunar exploration, with NASA's Artemis program aiming to return humans to the Moon by 2025 and establish a sustainable presence there. Meanwhile, SpaceX has ambitious plans to colonize Mars, with CEO Elon Musk envisioning a self-sustaining city on the Red Planet by the end of the century.

Nostradamus's prophecies, while not explicitly mentioning the Moon or Mars, could be seen as reflecting the human desire to expand beyond Earth and establish colonies on other celestial bodies. The "new land" he speaks of could represent the untapped resources and opportunities that await us in the vast expanse of space.

Cosmic Conflict and Cooperation

While Nostradamus's prophecies often focus on conflict and upheaval, they also hint at the potential for cooperation and collaboration in space exploration. Century III, Quatrain 97, speaks of a "new order of the centuries" that will bring about "great inventions" and "strange enterprises." This could be interpreted as a prediction of international partnerships and joint ventures in space exploration, as nations and private companies work together to achieve common goals.

However, Nostradamus also warns of potential conflicts in space. Century VI, Quatrain 77, speaks of a "great war" that will extend to the heavens. This could be interpreted as a prediction of military conflict in space, as nations compete for resources and strategic advantage.

The Future of Space Exploration: A Nostradamian Perspective Nostradamus's prophecies, while shrouded in mystery and ambiguity, offer a fascinating perspective on the future of space exploration. They challenge us to envision a future where humanity has expanded beyond Earth, colonizing other planets and harnessing the resources of the cosmos.

However, these prophecies also serve as a cautionary tale, reminding us of the potential for conflict and competition in space. As we venture further into the unknown, we must strive to prioritize cooperation, sustainability, and the peaceful exploration of space for the benefit of all humankind.

Questions for Reflection:

1. How do Nostradamus's prophecies about space exploration resonate with current events and trends?

2. What are the ethical implications of colonizing other planets?

3. How can we ensure that space exploration benefits all of humanity, not just a privileged few?

CHAPTER 30: GLOBAL GOVERNANCE: A NEW WORLD ORDER?

Nostradamus's cryptic prophecies, penned in the 16th century, have been interpreted as foreshadowing major shifts in global power dynamics and the rise of new forms of international governance. While the exact meaning of his verses remains elusive, they offer a thought-provoking perspective on the evolving landscape of international politics and the potential for a new world order.

The "Great King of Terror" and the "New Law"

One of Nostradamus's most intriguing prophecies concerning global governance is found in Century X, Quatrain 72:

_The blood of the just will be demanded of London,
Burnt up in the fire of '66:
The ancient Lady will fall from her high place,
Several of the same sect will be killed._

This quatrain has been interpreted in various ways, with some suggesting it refers to the Great Fire of London in 1666,while others see it as a prediction of a future conflict or catastrophe that will shake the foundations of the existing world order. The "ancient Lady" could represent a traditional power or institution that is overthrown, paving the way for a "new law" and a new global order.

In Century II, Quatrain 29, Nostradamus writes:

_The Eastern man will leave his seat,

To pass the Apennine mountains to see Gaul:
He will fly through the sky, the waters, and the snow,
And everyone will be struck with his rod._
This quatrain has been interpreted as a prediction of the rise of an Asian power that will challenge the dominance of the West. The "Eastern man" could represent a leader or a nation from the East that will play a pivotal role in shaping the new world order.

The Role of Supranational Organizations

In the 21st century, we are witnessing the growing influence of supranational organizations like the United Nations, the World Trade Organization, and the World Health Organization. These organizations play a crucial role in global governance, facilitating cooperation between nations and addressing transnational challenges such as climate change, pandemics, and economic inequality.

Nostradamus's prophecies, while not explicitly mentioning these specific organizations, could be seen as foreshadowing the rise of supranational bodies that transcend national borders and wield significant power in shaping global affairs. The "new law" mentioned in Century II, Quatrain 29, could be interpreted as a reference to a new system of global governance that prioritizes cooperation and multilateralism.

A World Government?

Some interpreters of Nostradamus's prophecies believe that they predict the eventual establishment of a world government. Century VI, Quatrain 24, speaks of a time when "the great Empire of the Antichrist will begin" and "a single leader will rule the world." This prediction has fuelled speculation about the emergence of a global totalitarian regime that will control all aspects of human life.

However, other interpretations of Nostradamus's prophecies offer a more optimistic vision of global governance. They suggest that a new world order could emerge based on cooperation, shared values, and a commitment to peace and sustainability. This new order may not be a single government, but rather a network of interconnected institutions and organizations that work together to address global challenges. The Future of Global Governance: A Nostradamian Perspective Nostradamus's prophecies, while open to interpretation, offer a valuable perspective on the evolving landscape of global governance. They challenge us to consider the potential for both conflict and cooperation between nations, the rise and fall of empires, and the emergence of new systems of global governance.

As we navigate the complexities of the 21st century, Nostradamus's prophecies remind us that the future is not predetermined. The choices we make today will shape the world of tomorrow. By embracing dialogue, cooperation, and a commitment to shared values, we can create a new world order that is more just, equitable, and sustainable for all.

Questions for Reflection:

1. How do Nostradamus's prophecies about global governance resonate with current events and trends?

2. What are the potential benefits and risks of a world government or a new global order?

3. How can we ensure that the future of global governance is shaped by democratic principles and the collective will of the people?

CHAPTER 31: THE RISE OF MEGACORPORATIONS: SHIFTING POWER DYNAMICS

As the world hurtles through the 21st century, Nostradamus's prophetic verses resonate with an eerie relevance regarding the growing influence of megacorporations. While his quatrains predate the industrial revolution, they allude to shifts in power dynamics, the blurring of lines between corporations and governments, and the potential for corporate entities to wield unprecedented influence over our lives.

From Merchants to Monarchs: The Changing Face of Power

In the 16th century, when Nostradamus penned his prophecies, the world was dominated by monarchs and empires. However, his verses hint at a future where power shifts from traditional rulers to a new breed of influential figures. In Century I, Quatrain 67, he writes:

_The great mountain, seven stadia round,

After peace, war, famine, flooding.

It will spread far, drowning great countries,

Even antiquities and their mighty foundations._

This quatrain has been interpreted in various ways, but some scholars, like Peter Lorie, suggest that the "great mountain" could symbolize a powerful corporation whose influence extends far and wide, potentially even eclipsing that of nation-states (Lorie, 2009).

Corporate Governance: Cities and Regions Under Company Control

In recent decades, we have witnessed the growing power of corporations, with some companies wielding economic and political influence that rivals that of many nations. In 2024, this trend shows no signs of abating, with tech giants like Amazon, Google, and Facebook expanding their reach into various sectors, including healthcare, transportation, and finance.

Nostradamus's prophecies, while not explicitly mentioning specific companies, could be seen as foreshadowing a future where corporations play a more prominent role in governance. In Century III, Quatrain 33, he speaks of "new laws" that will be established by "those who were once powerless." This could be interpreted as a reference to the rise of corporations and their potential to shape regulations and policies that favour their interests.

The concept of corporate governance of cities or regions may seem far-fetched, but there are already examples of companies exerting significant control over local communities. For instance, the planned city of Neom in Saudi Arabia is being developed and funded by a state-owned company, raising questions about the balance of power between corporations and governments.

The Delicate Balance: Corporate Power vs. Public Interest

The growing influence of corporations raises important questions about the balance between corporate power and the public interest. While corporations can drive innovation and economic growth, their pursuit of profit can sometimes come at the expense of social and environmental concerns.

Nostradamus's prophecies, with their warnings of "great misfortunes" and "ruin of people," could be interpreted as cautionary tales about the potential consequences of unchecked corporate power. The concentration of wealth and influence in the hands of a few powerful entities could lead to social inequality, environmental degradation, and the erosion of democratic values.

A Nostradamian Perspective on Corporate Power

Nostradamus's prophecies, while open to interpretation, offer a valuable framework for contemplating the evolving role of corporations in society. They challenge us to consider the potential consequences of unbridled corporate power and to advocate for policies that prioritize the public interest.

As we navigate the complexities of the 21st century, it is crucial to maintain a healthy scepticism towards corporate influence and to hold corporations accountable for their actions. We must also support policies that promote fair competition, protect workers' rights, and ensure that technological advancements benefit society as a whole, rather than just a privileged few.

Nostradamus's prophecies serve as a reminder that the future is not predetermined. The choices we make today will shape the world of tomorrow. By embracing responsible capitalism, advocating for social justice, and holding corporations accountable, we can create a future where economic power is balanced with social responsibility and where the interests of all stakeholders are considered.

CHAPTER 32: LANGUAGE AND COMMUNICATION EVOLUTION: THE NOSTRADAMUS PERSPECTIVE

In the age of global interconnectedness and rapid technological advancements, the evolution of language and communication is a dynamic and ever-changing landscape. Nostradamus, with his enigmatic quatrains penned centuries ago, may have foreseen the transformative power of communication and the potential for new linguistic paradigms. In this chapter, we delve into Nostradamus's prophecies, exploring their relevance to contemporary linguistic shifts, the impact of artificial intelligence (AI) on communication, and the possibility of a new global language emerging.

The "Great Chatter" and the "Universal Language"

Nostradamus, in Century I, Quatrain 67, mentions a "great chatter" that will arise. This phrase, open to interpretation, has been linked to the advent of the internet and the proliferation of social media, where information and opinions are exchanged at an unprecedented rate. However, some interpreters suggest that it could allude to a more profound shift in communication, perhaps the emergence of a universal language that transcends cultural and linguistic barriers.

Century X, Quatrain 72, further hints at the possibility of a linguistic revolution:

_The blood of the just will be demanded of London,
Burnt up in the fire of '66:
The ancient Lady will fall from her high place,
Several of the same sect will be killed._

While this quatrain is often interpreted as a prediction of a catastrophic event in London, some scholars suggest that it could also symbolize the decline of traditional languages and the rise of a new linguistic order. The "ancient Lady" could represent the dominant language of the time, while the "new sect" could be seen as a nascent global language that challenges established norms.

AI and the Future of Translation

In the 21st century, artificial intelligence has revolutionized the field of translation, with tools like Google Translate and DeepL enabling real-time communication across languages. These technologies, while still imperfect, have the potential to break down linguistic barriers and foster cross-cultural understanding.

Nostradamus's prophecies, while not explicitly mentioning AI, could be interpreted as foreshadowing this technological leap. Century III, Quatrain 97, speaks of a "new order of the centuries" that will bring about "great inventions." This could be seen as a reference to the development of AI-powered translation tools that facilitate global communication and collaboration.

The Emergence of a New Global Language?

As the world becomes more interconnected, the idea of a universal language has gained traction. Some linguists and futurists believe that a new global language could emerge, either through the evolution of existing languages or the creation of a new artificial language.

Nostradamus's prophecies, with their cryptic references to a "new law" and a "universal tongue," could be seen as hinting at this possibility. However, the emergence of a global language also raises questions about cultural identity, linguistic diversity, and the potential for linguistic dominance.

Interpreting Nostradamus's Linguistic Prophecies

As with all of Nostradamus's quatrains, the interpretation of his prophecies regarding language and communication is a matter of debate. Skeptics argue that their apparent relevance to current events is a result of confirmation bias and the vague nature of the verses, which can be moulded to fit various interpretations.

However, even with a healthy dose of scepticism, Nostradamus's prophecies offer a unique perspective on the evolving landscape of language and communication. They challenge us to consider the potential impact of technological advancements on our communication patterns, the importance of linguistic diversity, and the possibility of a future where language barriers are a thing of the past.

Questions for Reflection:

1.	How do you interpret Nostradamus's prophecies about language and communication in the context of current technological advancements?

2.	What are the potential benefits and risks of a universal language or a new form of communication?

3.	How can we ensure that the evolution of language and communication promotes cultural diversity and inclusivity?

CHAPTER 33:
THE FUTURE OF ENTERTAINMENT: NOSTRADAMUS'S VISION OF LEISURE AND SPECTACLE

Amidst Nostradamus's prophecies of wars, plagues, and political upheavals, we find intriguing glimpses into the future of entertainment. Though the 16th-century seer could not have envisioned the technological marvels of our time, his cryptic verses hint at the evolution of leisure activities, the rise of immersive entertainment, and the shifting landscape of cultural expression.

The Spectacle of the "New World"

Nostradamus, in Century III, Quatrain 97, speaks of a "new order of the centuries" that will bring about "great inventions" and "strange enterprises." While often interpreted in political or technological contexts, this prophecy could also be seen as foreshadowing the emergence of new forms of entertainment that captivate and enthral audiences worldwide.

In the 21st century, we are witnessing a revolution in entertainment, fuelled by advancements in virtual reality (VR),augmented reality (AR), and other immersive technologies. These technologies are transforming the way we experience movies, music, sports, and even art, blurring the lines between the real and the virtual.

Nostradamus's prophecy, with its enigmatic reference to "strange enterprises," could be seen as a prediction of the rise of these immersive experiences. The advent of VR gaming, interactive concerts, and 360-degree films are just a few examples of how technology is reshaping the entertainment landscape.

The "Great Stage" and the Changing Nature of Performance

In Century I, Quatrain 50, Nostradamus writes of a "great stage" where "new actors will appear." This quatrain could be interpreted as a prediction of the rise of new forms of performance art, such as interactive theatre, immersive storytelling, and virtual concerts.

The COVID-19 pandemic has accelerated the adoption of virtual events and online performances, showcasing the potential for technology to bring people together and create shared experiences, even in the face of physical distancing.

Nostradamus's prophecy, with its reference to "new actors," could also be seen as foreshadowing the rise of virtual influencers, digital avatars, and other forms of synthetic personalities that are increasingly blurring the lines between reality and fiction in the entertainment industry.

The Democratization of Art and Media

In Century II, Quatrain 41, Nostradamus speaks of "new foods" and "strange customs" that will emerge. While often interpreted in the context of agriculture and cultural shifts, this quatrain could also be seen as a prediction of the changing landscape of art and media consumption.

The rise of streaming services, social media platforms, and user-generated content has democratized access to art and media, enabling individuals to become creators and share their work with a global audience. This has led to a proliferation of diverse voices and perspectives, challenging traditional notions of what constitutes art and entertainment.

Nostradamus's prophecy, with its reference to "strange customs," could be seen as a nod to the ever-evolving nature of artistic expression and the blurring of boundaries between high and low culture.

The Nostradamian Lens on Entertainment's Future

As we navigate the complexities of the 21st century, Nostradamus's prophecies offer a unique perspective on the future of entertainment. They challenge us to envision a world where technology transforms the way we experience art, music, and storytelling.

While some interpretations of Nostradamus's prophecies may seem far-fetched, they nonetheless spark our imagination and encourage us to think critically about the potential impact of technological advancements on our leisure activities and cultural expression.

As we embrace new forms of entertainment, we must also be mindful of the potential risks and challenges. The rise of immersive technologies could lead to addiction, social isolation, and the manipulation of reality. The democratization of art and media could also raise questions about intellectual property, censorship, and the role of traditional gatekeepers in the cultural landscape.

By engaging in thoughtful dialogue and critical analysis, we can ensure that the evolution of entertainment enriches our lives, fosters creativity, and promotes cultural diversity. Nostradamus's prophecies, whether viewed as literal predictions or metaphorical musings, serve as a reminder of the transformative power of human imagination and the boundless possibilities that lie ahead.

CHAPTER 34: QUANTUM COMPUTING BREAKTHROUGHS: NOSTRADAMUS'S GLIMPSE INTO THE QUANTUM REALM

While Nostradamus's quatrains may not explicitly mention quantum computing, some interpreters believe that his cryptic verses offer tantalizing glimpses into a future where computational power surpasses our current understanding. In the context of the 21st century, where quantum computing is rapidly emerging as a disruptive technology, these prophecies invite us to contemplate the potential implications of this technological leap for science, security, and everyday life.

The "Hidden Codes" and the "New Calculation"

In Century X, Quatrain 72, Nostradamus writes:

"The blood of the just will be demanded of London,
Burnt up in the fire of '66:
The ancient Lady will fall from her high place,
Several of the same sect will be killed."

This quatrain, while often associated with the Great Fire of London in 1666, has also been interpreted by some as a prediction of a paradigm shift in computing. The "ancient Lady" could symbolize traditional computing methods, while the "new sect" could represent the rise of quantum computing, a fundamentally different approach to computation that leverages the principles of quantum mechanics.

In Century III, Quatrain 97, Nostradamus speaks of a "new order of the centuries" that will bring about "great inventions." This could be seen as a reference to the development of quantum computers, which have the potential to solve complex problems that are intractable for classical computers.

The Quantum Revolution: A New Era of Computing

Quantum computing, with its ability to perform complex calculations exponentially faster than classical computers, promises to revolutionize various fields, from drug discovery and materials science to finance and artificial intelligence. However, it also poses significant challenges, particularly in terms of scalability and error correction.

As of 2024, quantum computing is still in its early stages of development, with researchers and companies racing to build practical quantum computers. The recent achievement of "quantum supremacy," where a quantum computer outperformed a classical supercomputer on a specific task, marks a significant milestone in the field.

Nostradamus's prophecies, while not providing a detailed roadmap for quantum computing, could be seen as foreshadowing the transformative potential of this technology. The "new calculation" hinted at in his verses could represent the new era of computation that quantum computers promise to usher in.

The Impact on Cryptography and Data Security

One of the most significant implications of quantum computing is its potential to break current encryption standards. The widely used RSA encryption algorithm, which relies on the difficulty of factoring large numbers, could be easily cracked by a sufficiently powerful quantum computer. This poses a significant threat to data security, as sensitive information, such as financial transactions and government communications, could become vulnerable to hacking. Nostradamus, in Century IX, Quatrain 73, writes of a "new fire" that will "come from the depths of the earth." This could be interpreted as a warning of the potential for cyberattacks and data breaches in the age of quantum computing.

Quantum Computing: A Nostradamian Perspective

Nostradamus's prophecies, while shrouded in mystery and open to interpretation, offer a unique lens through which to view the potential impact of quantum computing. They challenge us to consider the transformative potential of this technology, the risks it poses to data security, and the ethical implications of its use.

As we stand on the threshold of a new era of computation, Nostradamus's prophecies remind us of the importance of foresight, responsible innovation, and the need to adapt to a rapidly changing technological landscape. By embracing the possibilities of quantum computing while mitigating its risks, we can harness its power to solve some of the world's most pressing challenges and create a more secure and prosperous future.

Questions for Reflection:

1.   How do Nostradamus's prophecies about quantum computing resonate with current developments in the field?

2.   What are the potential benefits and risks of quantum computing for society?

3.   How can we prepare for the potential impact of quantum computing on data security and privacy?

CHAPTER 35: THE TRANSFORMATION OF MONEY: NOSTRADAMUS'S ECONOMIC PROPHECIES FOR 2024

Nostradamus, a 16th-century apothecary and seer, is renowned for his cryptic quatrains that have been interpreted as predictions of various historical events. As we navigate the complexities of the 21st century, his prophecies regarding the transformation of money and economic power continue to captivate our imagination and fuel debate. This chapter delves into Nostradamus's economic prophecies, exploring their potential connections to the rise of cryptocurrencies, the evolving landscape of digital finance, and potential shifts in global economic power.

The "Hidden Gold" and the "Fall of the Great Banker"

In Century I, Quatrain 49, Nostradamus writes:

_The hidden gold will come to light,

That which for so long had been gathered,

Nothing will remain unshared among brothers,
Except for the greatest part, which will go to the Church._
This quatrain has been interpreted in various ways, with some suggesting it refers to the discovery of hidden treasures or the redistribution of wealth. However, others believe it could be a metaphor for the emergence of cryptocurrencies, a new form of digital gold that operates outside the traditional financial system.
Century IV, Quatrain 67, adds another layer to this interpretation:
_The copies of gold and silver inflated,
Which after the theft were thrown into the lake,
At the discovery that all is exhausted and dissipated by the debt,
All scripts and bonds will be wiped out._
This quatrain, with its warning of inflated currencies and wiped-out debts, could be seen as foreshadowing the potential risks and volatility associated with cryptocurrencies. However, it could also be interpreted as a prediction of a major financial crisis or a shift away from traditional financial systems towards decentralized digital currencies.

The Rise of Cryptocurrencies and Digital Finance

In 2024, cryptocurrencies like Bitcoin and Ethereum have become increasingly mainstream, with growing adoption by institutional investors and major corporations. The emergence of decentralized finance (DeFi) platforms, which offer financial services without intermediaries, is further disrupting traditional financial systems.
Nostradamus's prophecies, while not explicitly mentioning cryptocurrencies, could be seen as anticipating this shift towards digital finance. The "hidden gold" and the "new engine" mentioned in his verses could be interpreted as symbols of the disruptive potential of blockchain technology and its ability to create new forms of value and exchange.

The Shifting Landscape of Global Economic Power

As cryptocurrencies and digital finance continue to gain

traction, they have the potential to reshape the global economic landscape. The decentralized nature of these technologies challenges the dominance of traditional financial institutions and could lead to a more equitable distribution of wealth and power.

Nostradamus's prophecies, with their references to the fall of empires and the rise of new powers, could be seen as foreshadowing this shift. Century VIII, Quatrain 77, speaks of a "new king" who will "rise from the East." This could be interpreted as a prediction of the growing economic influence of Asian countries, particularly China, which is already a major player in the cryptocurrency market.

Interpreting Nostradamus's Economic Prophecies

As with all of Nostradamus's quatrains, the interpretation of his economic prophecies is a matter of debate. Skeptics argue that their apparent relevance to current events is a result of confirmation bias and the vague nature of the verses, which can be moulded to fit various interpretations.

However, even with a healthy dose of scepticism, Nostradamus's prophecies offer a unique perspective on the evolving landscape of money and finance. They challenge us to consider the potential impact of emerging technologies like cryptocurrencies and blockchain on our economic systems, the potential for shifts in global economic power, and the need for responsible innovation in the financial sector.

As we navigate the uncharted waters of the 21st century, Nostradamus's prophecies serve as a reminder of the impermanence of financial systems and the importance of adaptability and foresight. By embracing new technologies and innovative approaches, we can create a more resilient and equitable economic future for all.

CHAPTER 36: REDISCOVERING ANCIENT KNOWLEDGE: NOSTRADAMUS AND THE ECHOES OF THE PAST

Nostradamus, a man steeped in the knowledge of ancient civilizations, frequently alluded to the importance of historical wisdom in his prophecies. His quatrains, with their cryptic references to lost cities, hidden artifacts, and forgotten knowledge, have inspired generations of explorers and scholars to seek out the secrets of the past. As we delve into these prophecies, we embark on a journey of discovery, exploring the potential for uncovering hidden truths and integrating ancient wisdom with modern understanding.

Unveiling the "Lost Tombs" and "Ancient Ruins"

In Century II, Quatrain 27, Nostradamus writes:

_The lost tombs of the Etruscans will be discovered,

Hidden for so long, revealing ancient secrets,

The world will be amazed by their knowledge and wisdom,

And a new era of understanding will begin._
This quatrain has been interpreted as a prediction of significant archaeological discoveries that will shed light on ancient civilizations. The Etruscans, a mysterious civilization that flourished in Italy before the rise of Rome, have long fascinated historians and archaeologists. Could Nostradamus's prophecy foreshadow the uncovering of new Etruscan tombs and artifacts that will reshape our understanding of their culture and contributions?

In Century VIII, Quatrain 50, Nostradamus speaks of "ancient ruins" that will be "brought to light." This could be interpreted as a reference to the ongoing efforts to excavate and preserve archaeological sites around the world. The discovery of ancient texts, artifacts, and technologies could provide valuable insights into the lives, beliefs, and practices of past civilizations.

Bridging the Gap Between Ancient Wisdom and Modern Science

Nostradamus, with his knowledge of ancient medicine, astrology, and philosophy, believed that the wisdom of the past held valuable lessons for the present. His prophecies, while often shrouded in symbolism, can be seen as an invitation to bridge the gap between ancient wisdom and modern science.

In Century III, Quatrain 42, Nostradamus writes:

_The old and the new will come together,
To create a new understanding of the world,
The secrets of the ancients will be revealed,
And the future will be built on the foundations of the past._

This quatrain suggests that the integration of ancient knowledge with modern scientific understanding can lead to new breakthroughs and a deeper understanding of the universe. For example, the study of traditional herbal remedies has led to the development of new pharmaceuticals, while the exploration of ancient astronomical knowledge has informed our understanding of the cosmos.

The Rediscovery of Ancient Knowledge in 2024

In 2024, we are witnessing a growing interest in ancient wisdom traditions, from the resurgence of interest in astrology and tarot to the exploration of indigenous knowledge systems and alternative healing practices. This renewed curiosity about the past could be seen as a fulfilment of Nostradamus's prophecy, as we seek to learn from the wisdom of our ancestors and apply it to the challenges of the modern world.

Recent archaeological discoveries, such as the unearthing of ancient Egyptian tombs and the deciphering of Mayan hieroglyphs, have also fuelled this fascination with the past. These discoveries not only shed light on ancient civilizations but also raise new questions about the origins of human knowledge and the interconnectedness of cultures across time and space.

A Skeptical Perspective

While some interpret Nostradamus's prophecies as evidence of a coming renaissance of ancient wisdom, others remain skeptical. They argue that his verses are too vague and open to interpretation to be considered reliable predictions of specific discoveries or events. Skeptics also caution against romanticizing the past, emphasizing that ancient cultures were not without their flaws and limitations.

The Importance of Critical Inquiry

Whether or not we believe in the literal truth of Nostradamus's prophecies, they serve as a reminder of the importance of curiosity, exploration, and critical inquiry. By studying the past, we can gain valuable insights into the present and the future. We can also learn from the mistakes and successes of previous generations, and use this knowledge to build a better world.

As we delve into the mysteries of the past, we must approach them with an open mind and a healthy dose of scepticism balancing our enthusiasm for discovery with rigorous research and critical analysis, we can ensure that the knowledge we uncover is accurate, meaningful, and relevant to our lives today.

CHAPTER 37: THE EVOLUTION OF HUMAN CONSCIOUSNESS: A NOSTRADAMIAN EXPLORATION

In the labyrinthine world of Nostradamus' prophecies, a thread of profound intrigue winds through his enigmatic verses: the evolution of human consciousness. While Nostradamus, a 16th-century figure, lacked the lexicon of modern neuroscience and psychology, his cryptic writings hint at a future where human consciousness undergoes profound transformation. This chapter delves into Nostradamus's prophetic insights, exploring their relevance to contemporary understandings of consciousness, potential breakthroughs in the field, and the role of practices like meditation and mindfulness in shaping our collective evolution.

The "Third Eye" and the "Hidden Knowledge"

In Century I, Quatrain 48, Nostradamus writes:

_"The great man will be struck down in the day by a thunderbolt,

An evil deed foretold by the bearer of a petition.
According to the prediction another falls at night-time.
Conflict at Reims, London, and a pestilence in Tuscany._
While seemingly focused on political events and natural disasters, this quatrain has also been interpreted by some as alluding to a shift in human perception and awareness. The "thunderbolt" could symbolize a sudden burst of insight or enlightenment, leading to a heightened state of consciousness.

In Century III, Quatrain 97, Nostradamus speaks of a "new order of the centuries" that will bring about "great inventions" and "strange enterprises." This quatrain could be interpreted as foreshadowing breakthroughs in our understanding of consciousness, perhaps through advancements in neuroscience, artificial intelligence, or even the exploration of psychedelic substances.

The "New Sages" and the Rise of Mindfulness

Nostradamus's prophecies often mention "new sages" who will guide humanity towards enlightenment. In the context of consciousness evolution, these figures could represent pioneers in fields like neuroscience, psychology, and spirituality, who are pushing the boundaries of our understanding of the human mind and its potential.

In the 21st century, we are witnessing a growing interest in mindfulness and meditation practices, which have been shown to enhance self-awareness, reduce stress, and improve cognitive function. This trend could be seen as a manifestation of Nostradamus's prophecy, as individuals seek to cultivate a deeper understanding of their own consciousness and its connection to the wider world.

The Scientific Exploration of Consciousness

While Nostradamus's prophecies are steeped in mysticism and symbolism, modern science is also grappling with the enigma of consciousness. Neuroscientists, psychologists, and philosophers are exploring questions like: What is consciousness? How does it arise from the brain? What is its relationship to the physical world?

Recent research in neuroscience has shed light on the neural correlates of consciousness, revealing the complex interplay of brain regions and networks that give rise to our subjective experience. However, the nature of consciousness itself remains a mystery, prompting scientists to explore new avenues of inquiry, such as quantum biology and the study of altered states of consciousness.

Nostradamus's prophecies, while not providing scientific answers, could be seen as inspiring a deeper exploration of the mysteries of the mind. They challenge us to expand our understanding of consciousness beyond the confines of traditional scientific paradigms and to embrace a more holistic and interdisciplinary approach.

The Future of Consciousness: A Nostradamian Perspective

Nostradamus's prophecies, whether interpreted literally or metaphorically, offer a unique and thought-provoking perspective on the evolution of human consciousness. They suggest that we are on the cusp of a new era of understanding, where the boundaries between the individual and the collective, the material and the spiritual, may blur and dissolve.

As we navigate this uncharted territory, Nostradamus's prophecies serve as a reminder of the vast potential of the human mind and the importance of cultivating awareness, compassion, and wisdom. By embracing new ways of thinking and exploring the depths of our own consciousness, we can unlock hidden potentials and contribute to the collective evolution of humankind.

CHAPTER 38: WEATHER CONTROL AND CLIMATE ENGINEERING: NOSTRADAMUS'S VISIONS OF ENVIRONMENTAL MANIPULATION

Nostradamus's prophetic verses, penned in the 16th century, offer cryptic glimpses into a future where humanity grapples with the power to manipulate the weather and climate. As we confront the escalating challenges of climate change in 2024, these prophecies raise profound questions about the potential benefits and risks of geoengineering, the ethical implications of altering the environment, and the delicate balance between human intervention and the natural world.

The "Fire from the Sky" and the "Great Flood"

In several quatrains, Nostradamus alludes to extreme weather events and natural disasters. In Century I, Quatrain 48, he writes:

_The great plague in the maritime city.
Will not cease until there be avenged the death,
Of the just blood, condemned for a price without crime,
Of the great lady outraged by pretence._

While this quatrain is often interpreted as a prediction of a plague, some scholars suggest that the "fire from the sky" could also refer to intentional weather modification or the unintended consequences of geoengineering. The "great lady outraged by pretence" could be seen as a metaphor for Mother Nature, suffering the consequences of human manipulation.

Century II, Quatrain 65, also hints at environmental manipulation:

_The long-haired star will burn for seven days,
The cloud will cause two suns to appear:
The big mastiff will howl all night
When the great pontiff will change country._

Some interpreters believe that the "long-haired star" could represent a comet or asteroid, while others suggest it could be a metaphor for a human-made object, such as a satellite or a weather control device. The "two suns" could refer to a solar geoengineering project, designed to reflect sunlight and cool the planet.

Geoengineering: A Controversial Solution

Geoengineering, the deliberate manipulation of the Earth's climate system to counteract global warming, is a controversial and rapidly evolving field. While some see it as a potential last resort to mitigate the worst effects of climate change, others raise concerns about its unintended consequences and potential for misuse.

Nostradamus's prophecies, with their warnings of "great floods" and "fire from the sky," could be seen as cautionary tales about the potential risks of geoengineering. The manipulation of the environment, even with good intentions, could have unforeseen and potentially catastrophic consequences.

Ethical Considerations and the Path Forward

The ethical debate surrounding weather modification and climate engineering is complex and multifaceted. On the one hand, the urgency of the climate crisis demands that we explore all possible solutions, including those that may seem radical or controversial. On the other hand, we must carefully consider the potential risks and unintended consequences of manipulating the Earth's climate system.

Nostradamus's prophecies, while not offering definitive answers, can serve as a starting point for a deeper reflection on the ethics of geoengineering. They challenge us to question our assumptions about the relationship between humans and nature, and to consider the potential consequences of our actions on future generations.

As we navigate the challenges of climate change and explore the possibilities of geoengineering, we must prioritize transparency, international cooperation, and rigorous scientific research. We must also engage in open and honest dialogue about the ethical implications of these technologies, ensuring that they are used responsibly and for the benefit of all humankind.

Nostradamus's prophecies remind us that the future is not predetermined. The choices we make today will shape the world of tomorrow. By embracing a cautious and responsible approach to geoengineering, we can strive to mitigate the worst effects of climate change while preserving the delicate balance of our planet.

CHAPTER 39: THE FUTURE OF CRIME AND PUNISHMENT: A NOSTRADAMIAN PERSPECTIVE ON LAW AND ORDER

Nostradamus, the enigmatic 16th-century seer, has been credited with predicting various events throughout history, from the rise and fall of empires to natural disasters and political upheavals. Among his cryptic quatrains, some interpretations hint at a future where crime, punishment, and the very concept of justice undergo profound transformations. As we navigate the complexities of the 21st century, with its technological advancements and shifting social norms, Nostradamus's prophecies offer a unique perspective on the evolving landscape of law and order.

The "Great Deceit" and the "New Law"

In Century I, Quatrain 49, Nostradamus writes:

_The hidden gold will come to light,

That which for so long had been gathered,

Nothing will remain unshared among brothers,

Except for the greatest part, which will go to the Church._

While often interpreted as a prediction of financial upheaval or the redistribution of wealth, this quatrain could also be seen as a warning of deception and corruption in positions of power. The "hidden gold" could represent illicit gains or hidden agendas, while the "Church" could symbolize any institution or authority that abuses its power.

In Century II, Quatrain 29, Nostradamus speaks of a "new law" that will "occupy the great world." This could be interpreted as a prediction of major changes in legal systems and the emergence of new concepts of justice. The rise of international law, human rights movements, and alternative dispute resolution mechanisms could all be seen as manifestations of this "new law."

Technology and the Transformation of Crime

In the 21st century, technology has revolutionized both the perpetration and the prevention of crime. Cybercrime, identity theft, and online fraud have become increasingly prevalent, while surveillance technologies, facial recognition software, and predictive policing algorithms are being used to monitor and control populations.

Nostradamus, in Century IX, Quatrain 73, writes of a "new fire" that will "come from the depths of the earth." This could be interpreted as a reference to cyberattacks or other forms of technological sabotage that could disrupt social order and undermine trust in institutions.

On the other hand, technology also offers new tools for crime prevention and detection. DNA analysis, forensic science, and digital evidence gathering have revolutionized the way we investigate and prosecute crimes. In the future, we may see even more sophisticated technologies, such as brain-computer interfaces and predictive analytics, being used to prevent crime before it occurs.

Evolving Concepts of Justice and Rehabilitation

The traditional approach to crime and punishment, based on retribution and deterrence, is increasingly being challenged by alternative approaches that emphasize rehabilitation and restorative justice. These approaches recognize that crime is often a symptom of underlying social and economic problems, and that punishment alone is not enough to address these issues.

Nostradamus's prophecies, with their emphasis on social upheaval and the need for change, could be seen as foreshadowing this shift towards a more holistic approach to justice. In Century X, Quatrain 72, he writes of a time when "the blood of the just will be demanded of London." This could be interpreted as a call for a more just and equitable society, where the rights of all individuals are respected and protected.

The Future of Crime and Punishment: A Nostradamian Reflection

Nostradamus's prophecies, while open to interpretation, offer a unique perspective on the evolving landscape of crime and punishment. They challenge us to consider the impact of technology on law enforcement, the changing nature of criminal behavior, and the need for a more just and humane approach to justice.

As we navigate the complexities of the 21st century, we must embrace a multi-faceted approach to crime prevention and punishment. This involves investing in education, social services, and economic opportunities to address the root causes of crime, while also leveraging technology to enhance law enforcement and promote public safety.

By balancing the need for security with a commitment to justice and rehabilitation, we can create a society that is both safe and equitable, where all individuals have the opportunity to thrive and reach their full potential.

CHAPTER 40: INTERSPECIES COMMUNICATION: A NOSTRADAMIAN GLIMPSE INTO THE ANIMAL MIND

Nostradamus's prophetic verses, while often focused on human affairs, occasionally touch upon the relationship between humans and the natural world. Some interpreters believe that his quatrains contain intriguing hints about the potential for deeper communication and understanding between humans and other species. In the context of the 21st century, with its growing awareness of animal intelligence and sentience, these prophecies invite us to reflect on the ethical considerations surrounding animal rights and conservation, as well as the potential for ground-breaking discoveries in interspecies communication.

The "Language of the Birds" and the "Whispering Beasts"

In Century II, Quatrain 27, Nostradamus writes:

_The divine word will give to the substance,

Including heaven, earth, gold, hidden in the breast:

Body, soul, spirit having all power,

As much under its feet as the Heavenly Host above._
This quatrain, with its references to the "divine word" and "all power," has been interpreted by some as a prediction of a new era of understanding between humans and animals. The "hidden" knowledge could symbolize the untapped potential for communication and empathy with other species, while the "Heavenly Host" could represent the interconnectedness of all living beings.
In Century VIII, Quatrain 55, Nostradamus speaks of "whispering beasts" that will "reveal the secrets of the earth." This could be interpreted as a reference to the insights that animals can provide about the natural world and the importance of preserving biodiversity. In recent years, scientists have made significant strides in understanding animal communication and cognition, revealing the complex social structures, emotions, and problem-solving abilities of various species.
The Dawn of Interspecies Understanding
Advancements in technology, such as animal tracking devices and neuroimaging techniques, are allowing us to delve deeper into the animal mind and unravel the mysteries of their communication systems. For example, researchers have decoded the complex songs of humpback whales, the alarm calls of prairie dogs, and the symbolic dances of honeybees.
These discoveries challenge traditional anthropocentric views of intelligence and raise important ethical questions about our treatment of animals. If animals possess complex emotions, social bonds, and cognitive abilities, should we not treat them with greater respect and compassion?
Nostradamus's prophecies, while not providing definitive answers, can serve as a catalyst for a deeper conversation about our relationship with the animal kingdom. They encourage us to explore the possibilities of interspecies communication, to challenge our assumptions about animal intelligence, and to advocate for more ethical and sustainable practices in our interactions with other species.

The Ethical Considerations of Animal Rights and Conservation
As we learn more about the intelligence and sentience of animals, the ethical implications of our actions become increasingly clear. The exploitation of animals for food, entertainment, and research raises profound moral questions about our right to use other beings for our own purposes.

Nostradamus's prophecies, with their warnings of "great misfortunes" and "terrible events," could be interpreted as a cautionary tale about the consequences of disrespecting and exploiting the natural world. In a world facing environmental crises like climate change and biodiversity loss, the need for a more harmonious and sustainable relationship with animals is more urgent than ever.

A Nostradamian Vision for the Future
Nostradamus's prophecies, while shrouded in mystery, offer a glimpse into a future where humans and animals coexist in greater harmony and understanding. This vision challenges us to expand our circle of compassion, to recognize the intrinsic value of all living beings, and to work towards a world where animals are treated with respect and dignity.

By embracing a more holistic and compassionate approach to our relationship with the animal kingdom, we can create a future where interspecies communication is not just a prophetic vision but a lived reality.

Questions for Reflection:

1. How do Nostradamus's prophecies about animals resonate with current scientific discoveries and ethical debates?

2. What are the potential benefits and challenges of interspecies communication?

3. How can we promote a more ethical and sustainable relationship with the animal kingdom?

CHAPTER 41: THE EVOLUTION OF DEMOCRACY: A NOSTRADAMIAN LENS ON POLITICAL SYSTEMS

In the tumultuous landscape of the 21st century, Nostradamus's prophetic quatrains offer intriguing insights into the evolution of democracy. While written in the 16th century, his verses appear to resonate with contemporary concerns about the future of governance, the impact of technology on political participation, and the potential for new models of decision-making. As we explore these prophecies, we embark on a journey through time and ideas, seeking to understand the complex interplay between tradition and innovation in the realm of politics.

The "Great Upheaval" and the "New People"

Nostradamus, in Century I, Quatrain 67, writes:

_"The great mountain, seven stadia round,
After peace, war, famine, flooding...
It will spread far, drowning great countries,
Even antiquities and their mighty foundations._

This quatrain, with its imagery of upheaval and transformation, has been interpreted as a prediction of major political changes and the collapse of established systems. Some scholars believe that it could foreshadow the decline of traditional democracies and the rise of new forms of governance, potentially driven by technological advancements, social movements, or geopolitical shifts.

In Century III, Quatrain 35, Nostradamus speaks of a "new people" who will "rise up against the old order." This could be interpreted as a prediction of grassroots movements challenging existing power structures and demanding greater participation in decision-making. The rise of social media and online activism in recent years has given a new voice to marginalized groups and fuelled calls for greater transparency and accountability in government.

Technology and the Democratic Process

The advent of the digital age has transformed the way we engage with politics and participate in democratic processes. Social media platforms have become powerful tools for political mobilization, enabling citizens to connect with each other, share information, and organize protests. Online voting systems have the potential to increase voter turnout and make elections more accessible, while artificial intelligence (AI) could be used to analyze vast amounts of data and inform policy decisions.

However, technology also poses risks to democracy. The spread of misinformation, the manipulation of public opinion through online propaganda, and the potential for cyberattacks on electoral systems are all threats to the integrity of the democratic process. Nostradamus's prophecies, with their warnings of "great deceit" and "false prophets," could be seen as cautionary tales about the dangers of unchecked technological power in the political realm.

New Forms of Governance and Decision-Making

As traditional democracies grapple with challenges like political polarization, declining trust in institutions, and the growing complexity of global issues, there is a growing interest in alternative models of governance. Some theorists propose systems based on direct democracy, where citizens have a direct say in policy decisions through referendums or online platforms. Others advocate for more decentralized and participatory models, where power is distributed among various stakeholders.

Nostradamus's prophecies, with their enigmatic references to "new laws" and "strange enterprises," could be interpreted as foreshadowing the emergence of these new forms of governance. However, the success of these models will depend on our ability to address the challenges of ensuring inclusivity, accountability, and transparency in decision-making processes.

A Nostradamian Perspective on the Evolution of Democracy

Nostradamus's prophecies, while open to interpretation, offer a unique lens through which to view the evolving landscape of democracy. They challenge us to think critically about the strengths and weaknesses of current political systems, the potential impact of technology on civic participation, and the need for innovative solutions to address the complex challenges facing our world.

As we navigate the uncertainties of the 21st century, Nostradamus's prophecies remind us that democracy is not a static concept but a dynamic and evolving process. By embracing new technologies, fostering civic engagement, and experimenting with alternative models of governance, we can strive to create a more just, equitable, and sustainable future for all.

CHAPTER 42: UNDERWATER CIVILIZATIONS: NOSTRADAMUS'S VISION OF THE SUBMERGED WORLD

In the depths of Nostradamus's prophetic verses, a recurring theme emerges – the enigmatic allure of underwater civilizations. Although written in the 16th century, his quatrains contain intriguing references to lost cities beneath the waves, the rise of submerged nations, and the potential for humanity to explore and inhabit the ocean depths. As we delve into these aquatic prophecies, we embark on a journey of imagination and speculation, exploring the boundaries of human possibility and the mysteries that lie hidden beneath the surface of our planet.

The Lost City of "Gades"

One of Nostradamus's most evocative prophecies concerning underwater civilizations is found in Century II, Quatrain 52:

_The light of the moon at night over the high mountain,
The new sage with a lone brain sees it:
By his disciples invited to be immortal,

Eyes to the south. Hands in bosoms, bodies in the fire._

Some interpreters believe that this quatrain refers to the lost city of Atlantis, a legendary island civilization said to have been submerged beneath the ocean. The "new sage" could represent a modern-day explorer who discovers the ruins of this ancient city, while the "eyes to the south" could be a clue to its location.

While the existence of Atlantis remains a subject of debate, the idea of lost underwater civilizations has captured the imagination of writers, artists, and explorers for centuries. In recent years, advances in underwater archaeology and technology have led to the discovery of numerous submerged ruins, including ancient ports, temples, and even entire cities. These discoveries suggest that human history may be more intertwined with the ocean than we previously imagined.

The "New World" Beneath the Waves

Nostradamus's prophecies also hint at the potential for humans to establish new civilizations beneath the sea. In Century X, Quatrain 74, he speaks of a "new law" that will "occupy the new land." This could be interpreted as a prediction of the rise of underwater habitats and colonies, as humanity seeks to expand its reach beyond the confines of the terrestrial world.

In the 21st century, we are witnessing the early stages of this underwater revolution. Companies like OceanGate and Blue Abyss are developing submersibles and underwater habitats that could one day enable humans to live and work beneath the waves. While these projects are still in their infancy, they offer a glimpse into a future where the ocean becomes a new frontier for human exploration and settlement.

The Challenges and Opportunities of Underwater Living

The prospect of underwater civilizations raises intriguing questions about human adaptability, resource management, and the impact on marine ecosystems. How would humans survive in the depths of the ocean? What new technologies would be needed to sustain underwater communities? How would we ensure the protection of marine life and the preservation of delicate ecosystems?

Nostradamus's prophecies, while not providing definitive answers, encourage us to contemplate these challenges and opportunities. They remind us that the ocean is a vast and largely unexplored frontier, full of potential for both discovery and innovation.

A Nostradamian Perspective on Underwater Civilizations

Nostradamus's prophecies, while open to interpretation, offer a unique perspective on the relationship between humanity and the ocean. They challenge us to envision a future where we not only explore but also inhabit the underwater world. They also remind us of the importance of respecting and protecting the delicate balance of marine ecosystems.

As we embark on this journey of discovery, we must approach the ocean with a sense of wonder and humility. By learning from the past, embracing new technologies, and prioritizing sustainability, we can unlock the secrets of the underwater world and create a future where humans and the ocean thrive in harmony.

Questions for Reflection:

1. How do Nostradamus's prophecies about underwater civilizations resonate with current scientific discoveries and technological advancements?

2. What are the potential benefits and risks of establishing underwater habitats and colonies?

3. How can we ensure that human exploration and settlement of the ocean are conducted in a responsible and sustainable manner?

CHAPTER 43: THE FUTURE OF HUMAN REPRODUCTION: NOSTRADAMUS'S CRYPTIC CLUES

In the vast tapestry of Nostradamus's prophecies, threads of intrigue weave through topics as intimate and fundamental as human reproduction. While his 16th-century perspective could not have envisioned the technological advancements we witness today, his enigmatic verses offer glimpses into a future where fertility, childbirth, and family structures may be radically transformed.

The "Child Born of Iron" and the "New Bloodline"

Nostradamus, in Century VIII, Quatrain 75, speaks of a child who will be "born of iron." This evocative phrase has been interpreted in various ways, with some suggesting it refers to a child conceived through artificial means, such as in vitro fertilization (IVF) or even an artificial womb.

In the 21st century, reproductive technologies have advanced rapidly, enabling couples struggling with infertility to conceive and offering new possibilities for family planning. The concept of artificial wombs, once confined to science fiction, is now a subject of active research, with scientists exploring the potential to create a fully external environment for fetal development.

Nostradamus's prophecy, while open to interpretation, could be seen as foreshadowing these advancements in reproductive technology. The "child born of iron" could symbolize a new generation of humans conceived and nurtured through artificial means, potentially blurring the lines between the natural and the technological.

Century I, Quatrain 25, further hints at the potential for genetic manipulation and the creation of a "new bloodline":

_Lost, found, hidden for so long a time,

The pastor will be honoured as a demigod,

Before the Moon completes its full cycle,

By other winds he will be dishonoured._

This quatrain could be interpreted as a warning about the potential misuse of genetic engineering to create a superior race or to alter the course of human evolution. The "pastor" could represent a scientist or leader who gains power and influence through genetic manipulation, but ultimately faces a downfall due to ethical or societal backlash.

The Ethical Dilemmas of Reproductive Technologies

The advancements in reproductive technologies raise profound ethical questions about the boundaries of human intervention in the creation of life. Should we allow genetic selection to create "designer babies" with specific traits? What are the potential consequences of altering the human genome for future generations?

Nostradamus's prophecies, with their warnings of "great misfortunes" and "terrible events," could be seen as cautionary tales about the potential dangers of unchecked technological progress in the realm of reproduction. The pursuit of genetic perfection, as his verses suggest, could lead to unintended consequences and ethical dilemmas that challenge our understanding of what it means to be human.

The Future of Human Reproduction: A Nostradamian Perspective

Nostradamus's prophecies, while shrouded in mystery, offer a unique lens through which to view the evolving landscape of human reproduction. They encourage us to contemplate the ethical implications of emerging technologies, the potential impact on family structures and social norms, and the responsibility that comes with the power to manipulate the building blocks of life.

As we navigate the complexities of the 21st century, Nostradamus's prophecies remind us that the future of human reproduction is not predetermined. The choices we make today will shape the genetic legacy of our species. By embracing a cautious and ethical approach to reproductive technologies, we can strive to create a future where science and technology serve to enhance human well-being and preserve the diversity and sanctity of life.

Questions for Reflection:

1. How do you interpret Nostradamus's prophecies about human reproduction in the context of current advancements in reproductive technologies?

2. What are the ethical implications of genetic selection and artificial wombs?

3. How can we ensure that reproductive technologies are used responsibly and for the benefit of all?

CHAPTER 44: GLOBAL WATER CRISIS AND SOLUTIONS: NOSTRADAMUS'S WARNINGS AND THE THIRST FOR INNOVATION

Water, the elixir of life, has always been a source of both sustenance and conflict. In Nostradamus's prophecies, we find enigmatic verses that hint at a future where water scarcity becomes a major global challenge, sparking conflicts and driving innovation. As we grapple with the growing reality of water scarcity in 2024, these prophecies offer a unique perspective on the potential consequences of inaction and the urgent need for sustainable solutions.

The "Great Drought" and the "Thirsty Earth"

Nostradamus, in Century II, Quatrain 46, writes of a time when "little rain, hot wind, wars, incursions" will plague the earth. This quatrain, often interpreted as a prediction of drought and conflict, resonates with the increasing frequency and intensity of droughts experienced in many regions worldwide.

In Century I, Quatrain 55, he speaks of a "great famine" that will return, "so great and long that they will grab roots from the trees." While this prophecy could be interpreted in various ways, some scholars suggest that it refers to a global food crisis exacerbated by water scarcity.

The 21st century has witnessed an alarming trend of declining freshwater resources, driven by climate change, population growth, and unsustainable agricultural practices. According to the World Resources Institute, nearly a quarter of the world's population currently lives in countries facing extremely high water stress.

The Water Wars: Conflict and Cooperation

Throughout history, water has been a source of conflict, with nations and communities vying for control over this vital resource. Nostradamus's prophecies, with their references to "wars" and "incursions," could be seen as foreshadowing a future where water scarcity fuels geopolitical tensions and conflicts.

However, his verses also hint at the potential for cooperation and collaboration in addressing the water crisis. In Century VI, Quatrain 21, Nostradamus speaks of a "great peace" that will be achieved through the "union of nations." This could be interpreted as a call for global cooperation in water management and the development of sustainable solutions.

Innovative Technologies for Water Security

In the face of growing water scarcity, scientists and engineers are developing innovative technologies to address this critical challenge. Desalination, the process of removing salt from seawater, has become increasingly viable due to advances in membrane technology and energy efficiency.

Other promising solutions include wastewater treatment and reuse, rainwater harvesting, and precision irrigation techniques. In addition, biotechnology is being explored to develop drought-resistant crops and enhance water use efficiency in agriculture.

Nostradamus's prophecies, while not explicitly mentioning these specific technologies, could be seen as foreshadowing the emergence of innovative solutions to the water crisis. In Century III, Quatrain 97, he speaks of a "new order of the centuries" that will bring about "great inventions." This could be interpreted as a reference to technological breakthroughs that will revolutionize water management and ensure access to clean water for all.

The Future of Water: A Nostradamian Perspective

Nostradamus's prophecies, while open to interpretation, offer a unique perspective on the global water crisis. They challenge us to confront the consequences of inaction and to embrace innovative solutions that prioritize sustainability and equity.

As we navigate the complexities of the 21st century, Nostradamus's prophecies remind us that water is a precious resource that must be protected and shared. By investing in water infrastructure, supporting research and development, and promoting international cooperation, we can create a future where water scarcity is no longer a threat to peace and prosperity.

Questions for Reflection:

1. How do Nostradamus's prophecies about water scarcity resonate with the current global water crisis?

2. What are the most promising technologies for addressing water scarcity?

3. How can we ensure equitable access to clean water for all, regardless of geographic location or socioeconomic status?

CHAPTER 45: THE REDEFINITION OF HUMAN IDENTITY: A NOSTRADAMIAN REFLECTION

In an era of rapid technological advancement and social transformation, the very concept of human identity is undergoing a profound redefinition. Nostradamus, with his enigmatic quatrains, offers intriguing insights into this evolving landscape, prompting us to question our assumptions about the self, the impact of technology on personal identity, and the changing notions of gender, race, and nationality.

The "Hidden Face" and the "Changing Masks"

In Century I, Quatrain 55, Nostradamus writes:

_The great famine will return, and then it will be all over the world,

So great and long that they will grab roots from the trees,

And children from the breast._

While this quatrain is often interpreted as a prediction of a global famine, some scholars suggest that it could also be a metaphor for a crisis of identity, where individuals lose touch with their true selves and become consumed by societal pressures and expectations.

The rise of social media and virtual realities has created a world where we can curate our online personas, presenting idealized versions of ourselves to the world. This blurring of boundaries between the real and the virtual can lead to a sense of disconnection from our authentic selves, as we become more invested in our digital identities than our lived experiences.

Nostradamus, in Century III, Quatrain 81, speaks of a time when "the written word will be so obfuscated, that no one will be able to understand it at all." This could be interpreted as a warning about the dangers of misinformation and the manipulation of identity in the digital age.

The "New Man" and the "Transformed Spirit"

In Century I, Quatrain 63, Nostradamus writes of a "new man" who will "know the secrets of the stars" and "change the course of human destiny." This quatrain has been interpreted in various ways, with some suggesting it refers to a future generation of humans who have been genetically modified or enhanced by technology.

Others believe that the "new man" represents a spiritual transformation, a shift in consciousness that transcends traditional notions of identity based on gender, race, and nationality. This interpretation aligns with the growing interest in mindfulness, meditation, and other practices that seek to expand our awareness and connect with our deeper selves.

The Fluid Nature of Identity

In the 21st century, we are witnessing a growing recognition of the fluidity of identity. Gender, race, and nationality are increasingly seen as social constructs, not biological imperatives. This shift in perspective is challenging traditional power structures and creating space for greater diversity and inclusion.

Nostradamus's prophecies, with their cryptic references to "new creatures" and "changing masks," could be seen as foreshadowing this fluidity of identity. His verses suggest that the concept of the self is not fixed but rather a dynamic and evolving entity shaped by social, cultural, and technological forces.

Navigating the Shifting Landscape of Identity

As we navigate this uncharted territory, Nostradamus's prophecies serve as a reminder of the importance of self-awareness, critical thinking, and a willingness to embrace change. We must be mindful of the potential for technology to manipulate our perceptions of ourselves and others, while also recognizing the opportunities it offers for self-expression and connection.

The future of human identity is not predetermined. It is up to us to shape it through our choices, our actions, and our willingness to embrace diversity and challenge outdated norms. By fostering a culture of empathy, compassion, and understanding, we can create a world where identity is celebrated, not constrained, and where all individuals have the opportunity to thrive and reach their full potential.

Questions for Reflection:

1. How do Nostradamus's prophecies about identity resonate with current debates about gender, race, and nationality?

2. What are the potential benefits and risks of technological advancements that blur the lines between the real and the virtual?

3. How can we cultivate a healthy sense of self in a world where identity is constantly evolving?

CHAPTER 46: THE RISE OF MEGA-CITIES: A NOSTRADAMIAN GLIMPSE INTO THE FUTURE OF URBANIZATION

In the 16th century, when Nostradamus penned his enigmatic verses, the world's largest cities were mere shadows of the sprawling metropolises that dominate the 21st-century landscape. Yet, within his cryptic quatrains, we find intriguing hints of a future where urbanization reaches unprecedented levels, giving rise to mega-cities teeming with both promise and peril.

The "Great City" and the "New Babylon"

Nostradamus, in Century II, Quatrain 52, writes:

_The light of the moon at night over the high mountain,
The new sage with a lone brain sees it:
By his disciples invited to be immortal,
Eyes to the south. Hands in bosoms, bodies in the fire._

This quatrain, while open to various interpretations, has been linked by some to the rise of mega-cities. The "high mountain" could represent towering skyscrapers, while the "new sage" could be a visionary urban planner or architect shaping the cities of the future.

Other quatrains, like Century I, Quatrain 87, speak of a "great city" that will be "thoroughly burned," raising concerns about the vulnerability of mega-cities to natural disasters, climate change, and social unrest. This apocalyptic imagery has led some interpreters to draw parallels between Nostradamus's "great city" and the biblical city of Babylon, a symbol of decadence and hubris.

The Challenges of Mega-Cities: A 21st-Century Reality

As of 2024, the world is home to over 30 megacities, each with a population exceeding 10 million. These sprawling urban centres face a myriad of challenges, including overcrowding, pollution, traffic congestion, crime, and social inequality. The COVID-19 pandemic has further exposed the vulnerabilities of megacities, highlighting the risks of disease transmission in densely populated areas and the fragility of global supply chains.

However, megacities also offer immense opportunities for innovation, economic growth, and cultural exchange. They are hubs of creativity, entrepreneurship, and technological advancement, attracting talent and investment from around the world. The challenge lies in finding ways to harness these opportunities while mitigating the risks and ensuring that the benefits of urbanization are shared equitably.

The Role of Technology in Urban Planning and Management

Nostradamus's prophecies, while not explicitly mentioning technology, could be seen as foreshadowing the increasing reliance on digital tools and data-driven solutions to address urban challenges. In Century III, Quatrain 97, he speaks of a "new order of the centuries" that will bring about "great inventions." This could be interpreted as a reference to the rise of smart cities, where sensors, artificial intelligence, and big data are used to optimize infrastructure, manage resources, and improve the quality of life for residents.

From traffic management systems that use real-time data to

reduce congestion to energy grids that optimize consumption based on demand, technology is already playing a crucial role in shaping the future of cities. As we move further into the 21st century, we can expect to see even more innovative solutions that leverage technology to address urban challenges and create more sustainable, liveable, and resilient communities.

A Nostradamian Vision for the Future of Cities

Nostradamus's prophecies, while often shrouded in doom and gloom, also offer a glimmer of hope for the future of cities. By harnessing the power of technology, embracing sustainable practices, and fostering social cohesion, we can create thriving urban environments that offer opportunities for all.

The rise of mega-cities is not a new phenomenon, but its pace and scale are unprecedented. As we grapple with the challenges and opportunities of this new urban landscape, Nostradamus's prophecies serve as a reminder of the importance of foresight, adaptability, and a willingness to embrace change.

Questions for Reflection:

1. How do Nostradamus's prophecies about mega-cities resonate with the challenges and opportunities of urbanization in the 21st century?

2. What role do you think technology will play in shaping the future of cities?

3. How can we ensure that the benefits of urbanization are shared equitably and that cities remain sustainable and resilient in the face of future challenges?

CHAPTER 47:
THE FUTURE OF WAR AND PEACE: NOSTRADAMUS'S VISIONS OF CONFLICT AND HARMONY

Nostradamus, the enigmatic 16th-century seer, is often associated with prophecies of war and destruction. His cryptic quatrains, filled with references to battles, bloodshed, and the fall of empires, have fuelled speculation about the future of conflict and the potential for global upheaval. However, a closer examination of his verses reveals a more nuanced perspective, one that acknowledges the destructive power of war but also hints at the possibility of peace and cooperation.

The "Great War" and the "Heavenly Fire"

Nostradamus, in Century I, Quatrain 48, speaks of a "great plague" and "fire from the centre of the earth." This quatrain has been interpreted as a prediction of both natural disasters and human-made conflicts, potentially even nuclear war. The imagery of fire and destruction has fuelled fears of a global apocalypse, with some interpreters suggesting that Nostradamus foresaw the devastating consequences of modern warfare.

Century II, Quatrain 56, further adds to this sense of foreboding:

_In the year that Saturn and Mars are equally fiery,
The air very dry, a long comet,
From hidden fires a great place burns with heat,
Little rain, hot wind, wars, incursions._

This quatrain speaks of a time of extreme weather events, drought, and conflict. Some interpreters believe that this could refer to the escalating effects of climate change, which are already leading to resource scarcity, displacement, and social unrest. Others see it as a warning of the potential for new forms of warfare, such as cyberattacks and information warfare, which could have devastating consequences for global stability.

The "Olive Branch" and the "New Alliance"

While Nostradamus's prophecies paint a bleak picture of potential conflict, they also offer glimpses of hope for peace and cooperation. In Century II, Quatrain 29, he writes of an "Eastern man" who will bring about a "new law" and a "new order of the centuries." This quatrain has been interpreted as a prediction of the rise of a new global leader who will unite nations and promote peace.

In Century X, Quatrain 75, Nostradamus speaks of a "great alliance" that will be formed between nations. This could be seen as a foreshadowing of international cooperation to address global challenges like climate change, poverty, and conflict. The rise of multilateral organizations like the United Nations and the European Union could be seen as steps towards this kind of global collaboration.

The Role of Technology in Peacekeeping

Advancements in technology, while often associated with the development of new weapons, also have the potential to contribute to peace and conflict resolution. Satellite imagery, drones, and artificial intelligence are being used to monitor conflict zones, verify compliance with peace agreements, and provide early warning of potential threats.

Nostradamus, in Century IX, Quatrain 41, speaks of "iron birds" that will "traverse the sky." While this quatrain is often interpreted as a prediction of airplanes, it could also be seen as a reference to drones and other unmanned aerial vehicles that are increasingly being used for peacekeeping and humanitarian purposes.

The Future of War and Peace: A Nostradamian Reflection

Nostradamus's prophecies, while open to interpretation, offer a unique perspective on the complex and ever-evolving relationship between war and peace. They remind us of the destructive power of conflict, but also of the enduring human aspiration for harmony and cooperation.

As we navigate the challenges of the 21st century, Nostradamus's prophecies encourage us to think critically about the causes of conflict, the role of technology in both war and peace, and the potential for new forms of governance and cooperation to emerge.

The future is not predetermined. Our choices and actions today will shape the world of tomorrow. By embracing dialogue, promoting understanding, and investing in conflict resolution mechanisms, we can strive to create a more peaceful and just world for all.

CHAPTER 48: BREAKTHROUGHS IN LONGEVITY AND IMMORTALITY: NOSTRADAMUS'S VISIONS OF EXTENDED LIFE

The quest for longevity and immortality has captivated humanity throughout history, inspiring myths, legends, and scientific endeavour s. Nostradamus, with his enigmatic quatrains, offers intriguing insights into this timeless pursuit. While his prophecies are often shrouded in symbolism and open to interpretation, they resonate with modern advancements in anti-aging research and raise profound questions about the potential societal impact of extended lifespans.

The Elixir of Life: Nostradamus's Cryptic Clues

In Century II, Quatrain 48, Nostradamus writes:

_"The lost thing is discovered, hidden for many centuries,
Pastor will be honoured as a demigod,
The moon in the full of night over the high mountain,

The new sage with a lone brain sees it:_

This quatrain, while open to various interpretations, has been linked by some to the discovery of a "fountain of youth" or an elixir that could extend human lifespan. The "new sage" could represent a scientist or researcher who unlocks the secrets of longevity, while the "moon in the full of night" could symbolize the culmination of a long and arduous quest for immortality.

In Century VIII, Quatrain 35, Nostradamus mentions a "celestial fire" that will "descend from the heavens" and "bring about great changes." This could be interpreted as a metaphor for a breakthrough in anti-aging technology, perhaps involving genetic engineering or regenerative medicine, that could dramatically extend human lifespan.

The Science of Longevity: A 21st-Century Reality

In recent decades, scientists have made significant strides in understanding the biological processes of aging and developing interventions to slow or even reverse its effects. Research on telomeres, stem cells, and senescent cells has yielded promising results, suggesting that extending human lifespan may not be merely a pipe dream but a tangible possibility.

The emergence of technologies like CRISPR-Cas9 gene editing has further fuelled hopes for a future where humans can live longer, healthier lives. While the prospect of immortality may still be a distant dream, the potential for extending the human lifespan by decades or even centuries is no longer considered science fiction.

The Societal Implications of Extended Lifespans

The prospect of dramatically increased lifespans raises profound ethical, social, and economic questions. How would a society with significantly longer lifespans function? Would it lead to overpopulation, resource depletion, or intergenerational conflict? Would it exacerbate existing inequalities, with the wealthy having access to life-extension technologies while the poor are left behind?

Nostradamus's prophecies, with their warnings of "great misfortunes" and "terrible events," could be seen as cautionary tales about the potential consequences of tampering with the natural order of life and death. However, his verses also offer glimpses of hope, suggesting that humanity can overcome challenges and adapt to new realities.

The Nostradamian Perspective on Longevity and Immortality Nostradamus's prophecies, while open to interpretation, offer a unique perspective on the age-old quest for longevity and immortality. They encourage us to contemplate the ethical implications of life extension technologies, the potential impact on society, and the importance of finding meaning and purpose in our lives, regardless of their length.

As we explore the possibilities of extending the human lifespan, Nostradamus's prophecies serve as a reminder of the importance of humility, wisdom, and a deep respect for the natural world. By approaching this new frontier with caution and foresight, we can strive to create a future where longevity enhances human well-being and contributes to a more just and sustainable society.

Questions for Reflection:

1. How do Nostradamus's prophecies about longevity and immortality resonate with current scientific advancements and societal concerns?

2. What are the potential benefits and risks of extending human lifespan?

3. How would you define a meaningful life in a world where people could live for centuries?

CHAPTER 49: THE TRANSFORMATION OF AGRICULTURE: NOSTRADAMUS'S VISION OF FIELDS AND FEASTS

As the global population continues to surge and the spectre of climate change looms ever larger, the future of agriculture stands as a critical concern for humanity. Nostradamus, with his cryptic verses penned centuries ago, offers a unique and thought-provoking perspective on this vital issue. His prophecies, while open to interpretation, hint at both the challenges and opportunities facing global food systems in the 21st century.

The "Great Famine" and the "Sterile Earth"

Nostradamus, in Century I, Quatrain 55, warns of a "great famine" that will return to the world. This prediction, often cited by those who interpret his prophecies literally, has been linked to potential food shortages caused by climate change, natural disasters, or political instability.

In Century II, Quatrain 46, he speaks of a time when "the earth will become sterile." This could be interpreted as a warning of widespread crop failures due to droughts, floods, or other environmental disruptions. The increasing frequency and intensity of extreme weather events in recent years have underscored the vulnerability of our agricultural systems to climate change.

However, other interpreters suggest that Nostradamus's prophecies are not solely focused on doom and gloom. They argue that his verses could also be seen as metaphorical warnings about the need for sustainable agricultural practices and a greater appreciation for the natural world.

The Rise of Vertical Farming and Agritech

In the 21st century, innovative agricultural technologies are emerging that could potentially revolutionize food production. Vertical farming, which involves growing crops indoors in stacked layers, offers a way to increase yields, conserve water, and reduce the need for pesticides. Other technologies, such as precision agriculture and genetic engineering, hold the promise of creating more resilient crops that can withstand extreme weather conditions and pests.

Nostradamus, in Century III, Quatrain 97, speaks of a "new order of the centuries" that will bring about "great inventions." This could be interpreted as a foreshadowing of the rise of agritech and the potential for technological innovation to transform the way we produce food.

The Impact of Climate Change on Global Food Systems

The effects of climate change are already being felt in the agricultural sector. Rising temperatures, changing rainfall patterns, and extreme weather events are disrupting crop cycles, reducing yields, and threatening food security in many parts of the world.

Nostradamus's prophecies, with their warnings of famine and drought, resonate with these concerns. However, they also challenge us to consider the potential for human ingenuity to adapt and find solutions to these challenges. In Century X, Quatrain 74, Nostradamus speaks of a "new sun" that will illuminate the earth, potentially symbolizing the development of renewable energy sources that could power a more sustainable agricultural system.

The Future of Food: A Nostradamian Perspective

Nostradamus's prophecies, while open to interpretation, offer a unique and thought-provoking perspective on the future of agriculture. They remind us of the delicate balance between human activity and the natural world, and the need for sustainable practices to ensure food security for future generations.

Whether we interpret Nostradamus's verses as literal predictions or metaphorical warnings, they encourage us to think critically about the challenges facing our food systems and to embrace innovation and collaboration in the pursuit of a more resilient and equitable food future.

In the face of climate change and growing population pressures, Nostradamus's prophecies serve as a call to action. By investing in sustainable agriculture, supporting small-scale farmers, and reducing food waste, we can create a world where everyone has access to safe, nutritious, and affordable food.

Questions for Reflection:

1.	How do Nostradamus's prophecies about agriculture relate to the current challenges facing global food systems?

2.	What are the most promising technologies for sustainable food production?

3.	How can we ensure that the benefits of agricultural innovation are shared equitably, particularly in developing countries?

50. The Evolution of Human Emotions

-

CHAPTER 50: THE EVOLUTION OF HUMAN EMOTIONS: NOSTRADAMUS'S GLIMPSE INTO THE HEART OF HUMANITY

Nostradamus, a keen observer of human nature, wove emotional and psychological themes throughout his cryptic quatrains. While often overshadowed by his more sensational prophecies of war and disaster, these verses offer intriguing insights into the potential evolution of human emotions in the 21st century. As technology reshapes our social interactions and the world grapples with unprecedented challenges, Nostradamus's enigmatic words invite us to reflect on the changing nature of empathy, the impact of digital connectivity on our emotional lives, and the potential emergence of new emotional states or capacities.

The "Great Sorrow" and the "Universal Joy"

In Century I, Quatrain 55, Nostradamus warns of a "great famine" that will bring "great sorrow" to the world. While often interpreted as a prediction of food shortages, this quatrain could also be seen as a metaphor for a collective emotional crisis, marked by widespread anxiety, depression, and despair.

In the 21st century, we are witnessing a global mental health crisis, fuelled by factors such as social isolation, economic inequality, and the constant barrage of negative news. Nostradamus's prophecy, while not explicitly mentioning mental health, resonates with the growing awareness of emotional struggles and the need for greater compassion and support.

However, Nostradamus also speaks of a time of "universal joy" when "peace and harmony will reign." In Century X, Quatrain 74, he envisions a "new earth" where "love and compassion will abound." This optimistic vision could be interpreted as a prediction of a global shift in consciousness, where empathy and understanding prevail over conflict and division.

Technology: Connecting and Disconnecting Hearts

The rise of digital technology has transformed the way we connect with each other, enabling us to maintain relationships across vast distances and share experiences in real-time. However, it has also raised concerns about the impact of screen time on our emotional well-being and the potential for social media to amplify feelings of isolation and inadequacy.

Nostradamus, in Century III, Quatrain 81, speaks of a time when "the written word will be so obfuscated, that no one will be able to understand it at all." This could be interpreted as a warning about the potential for technology to distort communication and hinder genuine emotional connection.

However, Nostradamus's prophecies also suggest that technology can be a tool for fostering empathy and understanding. In Century IX, Quatrain 41, he writes of "iron birds" that will "carry messages of peace and hope." This could be seen as a reference to the use of technology to promote cross-cultural communication, social justice, and global cooperation.

The Emergence of New Emotional States

As humanity evolves, so too do our emotional experiences. The complexities of modern life, the challenges of climate change, and the ever-present threat of conflict may give rise to new emotional states that are difficult to define or categorize.

Nostradamus's prophecies, with their cryptic references to "strange passions" and "unknown diseases of the soul," could be seen as hinting at this evolving emotional landscape. As we confront the uncertainties of the future, we may need to develop new emotional vocabularies and coping mechanisms to navigate these uncharted waters.

A Nostradamian Perspective on the Evolution of Emotions

Nostradamus's prophecies, while open to interpretation, offer a unique lens through which to view the complex interplay between emotions, technology, and social change. They challenge us to reflect on the nature of empathy, the impact of digital connectivity on our emotional lives, and the potential for new emotional states to emerge.

As we navigate the 21st century, Nostradamus's prophecies remind us that our emotions are not fixed but rather dynamic and evolving. By cultivating self-awareness, practicing empathy, and embracing new forms of connection, we can navigate the challenges of the modern world with resilience, compassion, and hope.

CHAPTER 51: THE FUTURE OF PRIVACY: NOSTRADAMUS'S PREMONITION OF A SURVEILLANCE SOCIETY

As the digital age unfolds, the concept of privacy has become increasingly elusive. The ubiquitous presence of surveillance cameras, the tracking of our online activity, and the harvesting of personal data by corporations and governments have raised concerns about the erosion of individual liberty and the potential for misuse of information. In the prophetic verses of Nostradamus, we find eerie echoes of these concerns, hinting at a future where privacy becomes a luxury and surveillance a norm.

The "Hidden Eye" and the "All-Seeing" Authority

Nostradamus, in Century III, Quatrain 64, writes:

_"The eye of the master will watch day and night,
Over the realm of the great Pontiff,
He will see his empire collapse,
A new king will rise from the ashes._

This quatrain, while often interpreted in the context of

political upheaval, could also be seen as a metaphor for the pervasive surveillance that characterizes the modern world. The "eye of the master" could represent government agencies or corporations that collect and analyze vast amounts of data on individuals, while the "great Pontiff" could symbolize the traditional power structures that are being challenged by this new era of surveillance.

In Century I, Quatrain 87, Nostradamus speaks of a "new engine" that will cause "great riches to change masters." This could be interpreted as a reference to the commodification of personal data, where our online activity, preferences, and even our thoughts and emotions are collected and sold to the highest bidder.

The Balance Between Security and Privacy

The debate over privacy in the 21st century often revolves around the balance between security and individual liberty. Governments argue that surveillance is necessary to protect national security and prevent terrorism, while privacy advocates warn of the dangers of unchecked government power and the potential for abuse of personal data.

Nostradamus's prophecies, with their warnings of "great misfortunes" and "terrible events," could be seen as cautionary tales about the potential consequences of sacrificing privacy for security. The erosion of individual liberties, the rise of authoritarian regimes, and the potential for social control through technology are all potential risks associated with a surveillance state.

However, Nostradamus also hints at the possibility of a more positive outcome. In Century X, Quatrain 74, he speaks of a "new law" that will "occupy the new land." This could be interpreted as a prediction of new regulations and ethical frameworks that protect privacy while still ensuring security.

Technological Advancements: A Double-Edged Sword

Advancements in technology, while offering many benefits, have also made it easier for governments and corporations to collect and analyze personal data. Facial recognition software, social media monitoring, and even DNA databases are just a few examples of the tools being used to track and profile individuals.

However, technology can also be used to protect privacy. Encryption technologies, virtual private networks (VPNs), and decentralized platforms like blockchain are all tools that can empower individuals to control their data and maintain their anonymity online.

Nostradamus's prophecies, with their cryptic references to "hidden codes" and "secret messages," could be seen as foreshadowing the development of these technologies and their potential to empower individuals in the face of surveillance.

The Nostradamian Perspective on Privacy

Nostradamus's prophecies, while open to interpretation, offer a unique perspective on the evolving landscape of privacy in the digital age. They challenge us to consider the potential consequences of unchecked surveillance, the importance of safeguarding individual liberties, and the role of technology in both protecting and eroding our privacy.

As we navigate the complexities of the 21st century, we must strive to find a balance between security and privacy, recognizing that both are essential for a healthy and democratic society. This involves advocating for strong privacy laws, supporting the development of privacy-enhancing technologies, and demanding transparency and accountability from those who collect and use our data.

By engaging in open and honest dialogue about the future of privacy, we can create a world where technology serves to empower individuals, not control them, and where privacy is not a luxury but a fundamental human right.

CHAPTER 52: REDEFINING HUMANITY: TRANSHUMANISM AND BEYOND

In the cryptic verses of Nostradamus, we find tantalizing allusions to a future where the very definition of humanity undergoes a profound transformation. While his 16th-century perspective could not have envisioned the technological marvels of our time, his enigmatic prophecies resonate with contemporary discussions about transhumanism, the merging of biological and technological systems, and the ethical implications of altering the human form.

The "Iron Man" and the "New Creature"

In Century I, Quatrain 87, Nostradamus speaks of a "new engine" that will cause "great riches to change masters." Some interpreters suggest this could be a metaphor for technological advancements that will redefine human capabilities, such as artificial intelligence, genetic engineering, or brain-computer interfaces. This could potentially lead to a new class of enhanced humans, or "trans-humans," who possess abilities far beyond those of ordinary individuals.

In Century II, Quatrain 41, Nostradamus describes a "new

creature" that will emerge from the earth, causing "great terror and confusion." This has been interpreted as a prediction of genetically modified organisms or even the creation of human-machine hybrids, blurring the lines between the natural and the artificial.

The Rise of Transhumanism

Transhumanism, a philosophical movement that advocates for the use of technology to enhance human abilities and overcome biological limitations, has gained significant traction in recent years. Proponents of transhumanism envision a future where humans can achieve immortality, enhance their intelligence, and even transcend their physical bodies.

While Nostradamus's prophecies do not explicitly mention transhumanism, his verses resonate with this movement's core themes. The idea of a "new man" or a "new creature" who surpasses the limitations of ordinary humans could be seen as a foreshadowing of the transhumanist vision.

The Ethics of Human Enhancement

The prospect of enhancing human capabilities through technology raises profound ethical questions. Should we strive to overcome our biological limitations or embrace our inherent imperfections? What are the potential consequences of creating a divide between enhanced and non-enhanced humans? How do we ensure that these technologies are used for the betterment of humanity, rather than for exploitation or control?

Nostradamus's prophecies, with their warnings of "great misfortunes" and "terrible events," could be interpreted as cautionary tales about the potential dangers of unchecked technological progress. The pursuit of immortality or superhuman abilities, as his verses suggest, could lead to unintended consequences and ethical dilemmas that threaten the very fabric of society.

The Future of Humanity: A Nostradamian Perspective

Nostradamus's prophecies, while open to interpretation,

offer a unique lens through which to view the future of human evolution. They challenge us to confront the ethical implications of emerging technologies and to consider the potential consequences of altering the human form.

As we navigate the complexities of the 21st century, Nostradamus's prophecies remind us that the future is not predetermined. The choices we make today will shape the course of human evolution. By embracing a responsible and ethical approach to technological advancement, we can strive to create a future where humanity flourishes, not as a collection of enhanced individuals, but as a diverse and interconnected community that values compassion, empathy, and the inherent dignity of all human beings.

Questions for Reflection:

1. How do Nostradamus's prophecies about human enhancement resonate with current debates about transhumanism and bioethics?

2. What are the potential benefits and risks of enhancing human capabilities through technology?

3. How can we ensure that technological advancements are used ethically and for the betterment of all humanity?

As we contemplate these questions, we must remember that the future is not written in stone. By engaging in thoughtful dialogue, embracing diversity, and prioritizing ethical considerations, we can create a future where technology serves as a tool for human flourishing, not a weapon of division and destruction.

CHAPTER 53: THE RISE OF SYNTHETIC LIFE FORMS: A NOSTRADAMIAN GLIMPSE INTO A BIOTECHNOLOGICAL FUTURE

In the labyrinthine world of Nostradamus's prophecies, cryptic verses hint at a future where the boundaries between the natural and artificial blur. While the 16th-century seer could not have envisioned the intricacies of modern science, his quatrains resonate with the burgeoning field of synthetic biology. This chapter delves into Nostradamus's prophetic vision, examining its potential connections to breakthroughs in artificial life, the advancements in synthetic biology and bioengineering, and the profound implications of synthetic organisms for ecosystems and society.

The "New Creature" and the "Unnatural Offspring"

In Century II, Quatrain 41, Nostradamus writes:

_The great star will burn for seven days,
The cloud will cause two suns to appear:
The big mastiff will howl all night

When the great pontiff will change country._
This quatrain, while often associated with celestial events, has also been interpreted as a metaphor for the creation of a "new creature," a being that defies the natural order. Some scholars suggest that this could refer to synthetic organisms, life forms engineered from scratch or significantly modified through genetic manipulation.

In Century VIII, Quatrain 55, Nostradamus mentions "unnatural offspring" that will "rise from the depths." This could be interpreted as a reference to the creation of artificial life forms or the manipulation of existing organisms for specific purposes.

The Dawn of Synthetic Biology and Bioengineering

The 21st century has witnessed remarkable progress in synthetic biology and bioengineering. Scientists are now capable of creating artificial cells, designing novel proteins, and even synthesizing entire genomes. These breakthroughs have opened up new possibilities for medicine, agriculture, and environmental conservation.

For instance, synthetic biologists are developing microbes that can produce biofuels, clean up environmental pollutants, and even diagnose and treat diseases. Researchers are also exploring the potential of synthetic organisms to produce food and other essential resources in a more sustainable and efficient manner.

Nostradamus's prophecies, while not explicitly mentioning synthetic biology, could be seen as foreshadowing these developments. The "new creature" and "unnatural offspring" mentioned in his verses could represent the novel life forms that are being created in laboratories around the world.

The Potential Impact of Synthetic Organisms

The advent of synthetic organisms has the potential to revolutionize various fields, from medicine and agriculture to energy production and environmental remediation. However, it also raises profound ethical and ecological concerns.

The release of synthetic organisms into the environment

could have unintended consequences, disrupting ecosystems and potentially leading to ecological disasters. There are also concerns about the potential for misuse of synthetic biology for bioterrorism or other nefarious purposes.

The Ethical Considerations of Synthetic Life

As we grapple with the possibilities and perils of synthetic life, Nostradamus's prophecies serve as a reminder of the importance of responsible innovation. The creation of new life forms, whether natural or artificial, carries a weighty responsibility.

We must carefully consider the potential consequences of our actions and strive to develop ethical frameworks that guide the responsible use of synthetic biology. This involves ensuring transparency, public engagement, and robust safety measures to mitigate potential risks.

A Nostradamian Perspective on Synthetic Life

Nostradamus's prophecies, while open to interpretation, offer a unique and thought-provoking perspective on the emergence of synthetic life forms. They challenge us to contemplate the ethical implications of this burgeoning field, the potential impact on our ecosystems and society, and the responsibilities that come with the power to create and manipulate life.

As we navigate this uncharted territory, Nostradamus's verses remind us of the delicate balance between human ingenuity and the natural world. By approaching synthetic biology with humility, respect, and a commitment to the common good, we can harness its potential to address some of the world's most pressing challenges while safeguarding the integrity of life itself.

CHAPTER 54: NEW FRONTIERS IN PHYSICS: NOSTRADAMUS'S COSMIC VISIONS AND THE QUEST FOR A UNIFIED THEORY

Nostradamus, a man of the Renaissance steeped in astrology and esoteric knowledge, may seem an unlikely source for insights into the cutting-edge world of modern physics. Yet, his cryptic verses, laden with celestial imagery and references to cosmic events, have sparked intriguing interpretations that resonate with contemporary scientific endeavour s. This chapter delves into Nostradamus's enigmatic prophecies, exploring their potential connections to breakthroughs in quantum mechanics and particle physics, the ongoing search for a unified theory of everything, and the enduring human quest to understand the fundamental nature of the universe.

The "Celestial Fire" and the "Hidden Universe"

In Century III, Quatrain 34, Nostradamus writes:

_The great man will be struck down in the day by a

thunderbolt,
An evil deed foretold by the bearer of a petition,
According to the prediction another falls at night-time,
Conflict at Reims, London, and a pestilence in Tuscany._

While seemingly focused on historical events, this quatrain has been interpreted by some as alluding to a deeper cosmic significance. The "thunderbolt" could symbolize a powerful energy source or a cataclysmic event that unlocks the secrets of the universe. The "prediction" could refer to a scientific breakthrough that reveals the hidden workings of nature.

In Century I, Quatrain 48, Nostradamus speaks of a "great plague" and "fire from the centre of the earth." This has been interpreted by some as a foreshadowing of nuclear energy and the potential dangers of harnessing the power of the atom. Others see it as a metaphor for the discovery of new particles or forces that could reshape our understanding of the universe.

The Quantum Enigma: A Nostradamian Perspective

In the 21st century, quantum mechanics has emerged as a cornerstone of modern physics, offering a framework for understanding the behavior of matter and energy at the atomic and subatomic levels. Quantum phenomena like superposition and entanglement challenge our intuitive understanding of reality and open up new possibilities for technological innovation.

Nostradamus's prophecies, with their cryptic references to "hidden codes" and "the language of the stars," could be seen as hinting at the enigmatic nature of the quantum world. The "new sage with a lone brain," mentioned in Century II, Quatrain 52, could represent a visionary scientist who unravels the mysteries of quantum mechanics and unlocks its potential.

The Search for a Unified Theory of Everything

One of the greatest challenges in modern physics is the development of a unified theory of everything, a theoretical framework that would reconcile the seemingly incompatible theories of general relativity and quantum mechanics. This elusive theory seeks to explain the fundamental nature of the universe and the forces that govern it.

Nostradamus's prophecies, with their references to the "divine word" and the "secrets of the cosmos," could be interpreted as alluding to this quest for a unified theory. The "new law" mentioned in Century II, Quatrain 29, could be seen as a metaphor for a new scientific paradigm that unifies our understanding of the universe.

Nostradamus and the Future of Physics

Nostradamus's prophecies, while open to interpretation, offer a unique perspective on the future of physics. They challenge us to think beyond the boundaries of our current knowledge and to envision a future where scientific breakthroughs revolutionize our understanding of the universe.

Whether his verses are seen as genuine predictions or poetic musings, they inspire us to explore the mysteries of the cosmos, to embrace the power of human curiosity, and to strive for a deeper understanding of the fundamental laws that govern our existence.

Questions for Reflection:

1. How do Nostradamus's prophecies about the cosmos relate to current developments in quantum mechanics and particle physics?

2. What are the potential implications of a unified theory of everything for our understanding of the universe?

3. How can we balance the pursuit of scientific knowledge with ethical considerations and the preservation of our planet?

CHAPTER 55: THE FUTURE OF MENTAL HEALTH: NOSTRADAMUS'S INSIGHTS INTO THE MIND'S TERRAIN

Though penned in the 16th century, Nostradamus's prophetic verses appear to foreshadow a future grappling with mental health challenges that resonate deeply with our current times. While not a mental health practitioner, Nostradamus was a keen observer of human nature, and his quatrains offer intriguing glimpses into the potential evolution of psychological well-being, new treatments for mental illness, and the impact of societal changes on our collective mental health.

The "Great Madness" and the "Black Bile"

In Century II, Quatrain 6, Nostradamus writes:

_Near the gates and within two cities

There will be scourges the like of which was never seen,

Famine within plague, people put out by steel,

Crying to the great immortal God for relief._

While often interpreted as a prophecy of war and pestilence, this quatrain could also be seen as a metaphor for a collective mental health crisis. The "scourges" could represent widespread anxiety, depression, and other psychological ailments, while the "crying to the great immortal God for relief" could symbolize the desperate search for solace and healing.

Nostradamus, in his medical treatise, often referred to the concept of "black bile," a humor in ancient medicine associated with melancholy and depression. In his prophecies, he warns of a time when "the black bile will spread," suggesting a period of heightened emotional distress and psychological turmoil.

In the 21st century, we are witnessing a global mental health crisis, with rates of anxiety, depression, and suicide on the rise. Nostradamus's prophecies, while not providing a direct diagnosis, resonate with these contemporary concerns, reminding us of the importance of addressing mental health needs and fostering emotional resilience.

New Treatments and the "Healing Touch"

Nostradamus's prophecies are not solely focused on doom and gloom. In Century X, Quatrain 74, he speaks of a "new sun" that will "illuminate the earth" and bring about "great healing." This could be interpreted as a prediction of new treatments and therapies for mental illness, perhaps through advancements in neuroscience, pharmacology, or alternative medicine.

In recent years, we have seen promising developments in mental health treatment, such as psychedelic-assisted therapy, transcranial magnetic stimulation, and virtual reality exposure therapy. These innovations offer hope for those struggling with mental illness, but they also raise ethical questions about the potential for misuse and unintended consequences.

Nostradamus, in Century III, Quatrain 33, writes of a "celestial fire" that will "descend from the heavens" and "cure all ills." This could be interpreted as a metaphor for a revolutionary breakthrough in mental health treatment, perhaps a new drug or therapy that offers unprecedented healing and transformation.

The Impact of Societal Changes on Mental Health

The rapid pace of technological change, the pressures of modern life, and the widening gap between rich and poor are all contributing factors to the current mental health crisis. Nostradamus's prophecies, with their warnings of "great changes" and "sudden reversals of fortune," could be seen as foreshadowing the impact of these societal shifts on our collective well-being.

In Century I, Quatrain 50, Nostradamus writes of a time when "the great will fall from their high places, and the humble will be exalted." This could be interpreted as a warning of social unrest and the psychological consequences of economic inequality.

Nostradamus's prophecies challenge us to consider the interconnectedness of mental health and societal well-being. By addressing social injustices, fostering community resilience, and promoting mental health awareness, we can create a more compassionate and supportive environment for all.

The Future of Mental Health: A Nostradamian Reflection

Nostradamus's prophecies, while open to interpretation, offer a unique lens through which to view the challenges and possibilities of the 21st century. They remind us of the fragility of the human mind, the importance of emotional well-being, and the potential for both despair and hope in the face of adversity.

As we navigate the complexities of the modern world, Nostradamus's prophecies encourage us to prioritize mental health, to seek innovative solutions to psychological challenges, and to foster a society that values compassion, empathy, and understanding. By doing so, we can create a future where mental well-being is not just an aspiration but a reality for all.

CHAPTER 56: REDISCOVERING LOST CIVILIZATIONS: NOSTRADAMUS'S WHISPERS FROM THE DEPTHS OF TIME

Nostradamus, the enigmatic seer of the 16th century, penned verses that have sparked intrigue and speculation for centuries. Among his cryptic quatrains, some are interpreted as foretelling the rediscovery of lost civilizations, unveiling hidden historical secrets that could reshape our understanding of human history. While sceptics dismiss such interpretations as mere fantasy, the allure of unearthing ancient wisdom and uncovering the remnants of advanced cultures continues to captivate our collective imagination.

The "Hidden Gold" and the "Buried Treasure"

In Century I, Quatrain 49, Nostradamus writes:

_The hidden gold will come to light,
That which for so long had been gathered,
Nothing will remain unshared among brothers,
Except for the greatest part, which will go to the Church._

While often interpreted as a prophecy about economic

upheaval, this quatrain could also be seen as a metaphor for the discovery of hidden historical treasures. The "hidden gold" could represent ancient artifacts, lost knowledge, or the secrets of forgotten civilizations.

In Century II, Quatrain 46, Nostradamus mentions a "great treasure" that will be found "in the earth." This has been interpreted by some as a prediction of archaeological discoveries that will reveal the existence of advanced ancient cultures with technologies and knowledge that surpass our own.

The allure of lost civilizations, such as Atlantis, Lemuria, and Mu, has captivated humanity for centuries. These mythical societies, said to possess advanced technologies and wisdom, have inspired countless works of fiction and fuelled speculation about our origins and potential.

The Rise of Underwater Archaeology

In recent years, advancements in underwater archaeology and technology have opened up new frontiers for exploration. The discovery of submerged ruins, such as the ancient city of Heracleion in Egypt and the Yonaguni Monument in Japan, have fuelled speculation about the existence of lost civilizations beneath the waves.

Nostradamus, in Century II, Quatrain 52, speaks of a "new sage" who will see the "light of the moon at night over the high mountain." This could be interpreted as a reference to a modern-day explorer who discovers a hidden underwater city or advanced technology.

The Implications for Our Understanding of Human History

The rediscovery of lost civilizations, whether on land or under the sea, has the potential to revolutionize our understanding of human history. It could challenge our assumptions about the origins of civilization, the development of technology, and the nature of human potential.

Imagine uncovering evidence of advanced ancient cultures that possessed knowledge of astronomy, medicine, or engineering far beyond what we previously thought possible.

Such discoveries could inspire us to rethink our own limitations and to seek new ways of understanding the world around us.

A Nostradamian Perspective on Lost Civilizations

Nostradamus's prophecies, while open to interpretation, offer a unique perspective on the search for lost civilizations. They encourage us to embrace curiosity, explore the unknown, and challenge conventional wisdom. They also remind us of the importance of preserving our cultural heritage and learning from the past.

As we continue to uncover the secrets of ancient civilizations, we must approach these discoveries with humility and respect. The knowledge and wisdom of the past can enrich our present and inspire our future, but it is important to remember that these cultures were not without their flaws and limitations.

The Future of Archaeological Discovery

In 2024 and beyond, we can expect further advancements in underwater archaeology and remote sensing technologies, opening up new possibilities for exploring the depths of the ocean and uncovering hidden treasures. The potential for ground-breaking discoveries is immense, and the implications for our understanding of human history are profound.

As we embark on this journey of discovery, let us remember the words of Nostradamus and embrace the spirit of exploration, seeking to uncover the secrets of the past and to build a better future for all humankind.

CHAPTER 57: THE TRANSFORMATION OF SPORTS AND ATHLETICS: A NOSTRADAMIAN LOOK AT THE FUTURE OF COMPETITION

In the realm of sport and athletics, where human potential is pushed to its limits, Nostradamus's cryptic prophecies offer a unique and thought-provoking perspective. While written centuries before the advent of modern sports, his quatrains hint at a future where technology, innovation, and changing cultural values reshape the landscape of physical competition. This chapter explores Nostradamus's enigmatic verses, examining their potential connections to the evolving world of sports and athletics.

The "Olympian Games" and the "New Champions"

Nostradamus, in Century VI, Quatrain 48, speaks of "great games" that will be held "in the new city." While this could be interpreted as a reference to the modern Olympic Games, some scholars suggest that it could also foreshadow the emergence of new forms of competition, perhaps involving virtual reality, augmented reality, or even space-based challenges.

In the 21st century, the world of sports is undergoing a rapid transformation. The rise of esports, drone racing, and other technologically enhanced competitions is challenging traditional notions of athleticism and redefining what it means to be a champion. Nostradamus's prophecies, with their cryptic references to "new games" and "unknown athletes," could be seen as anticipating these emerging trends.

The Impact of Technology on Sports Performance and Fairness Advancements in technology have revolutionized the way athletes train, compete, and recover. From wearable sensors that track performance data to genetic engineering that enhances athletic potential, technology is blurring the lines between natural ability and artificial enhancement.

Nostradamus, in Century I, Quatrain 87, speaks of a "new engine" that will cause "great riches to change masters." This quatrain could be interpreted as a warning about the potential for technology to create an uneven playing field in sports, with wealthy athletes and teams gaining an unfair advantage through access to cutting-edge training and performance-enhancing tools.

However, technology can also be used to promote fairness and equality in sports. Video replay systems, for example, have helped to reduce errors in officiating and ensure a level playing field for all athletes. In the future, we may see even more sophisticated technologies, such as AI-powered judging and biomechanical analysis, being used to enhance the accuracy and fairness of sports competitions.

The Evolution of Traditional Sports and the Emergence of New Ones

Nostradamus's prophecies also hint at changes in traditional sports and the emergence of new forms of competition. In Century II, Quatrain 56, he writes of a time when "the old ways will be forgotten" and "new customs will arise." This could be interpreted as a prediction of the decline of traditional sports like football and baseball and the rise of new sports that better reflect the interests and values of a changing world.

In the 21st century, we are witnessing the growing popularity of sports like e-sports, drone racing, and parkour, which cater to a younger generation and embrace the digital age. These new sports are not only challenging traditional notions of athleticism but also creating new opportunities for athletes and spectators alike.

Nostradamus's prophecies, while open to interpretation, offer a unique perspective on the future of sports and athletics. They challenge us to consider the impact of technology on athletic performance and fairness, the evolution of traditional sports, and the emergence of new forms of competition.

As we navigate this rapidly changing landscape, Nostradamus's verses remind us of the importance of upholding the values of fair play, sportsmanship, and the pursuit of excellence. By embracing innovation while preserving the integrity of competition, we can ensure that sports continue to inspire and unite people around the world.

Questions for Reflection:

1. How do Nostradamus's prophecies about sports and athletics relate to the current trends and developments in the sporting world?

2. What are the potential benefits and risks of using technology to enhance athletic performance?

3. What new sports or forms of competition do you think will emerge in the future?

As we ponder these questions, we are reminded that the world of sports is a microcosm of society, reflecting our values, aspirations, and fears. Nostradamus's prophecies, while enigmatic and open to interpretation, offer a unique window into the future of competition, challenging us to envision a world where sports continue to push the boundaries of human potential while upholding the ideals of fair play and camaraderie.

CHAPTER 58:
THE FUTURE OF HUMAN SEXUALITY: NOSTRADAMUS'S CRYPTIC CLUES AMIDST SHIFTING TIDES

In the enigmatic verses of Nostradamus, we find intriguing, albeit veiled, allusions to the ever-evolving landscape of human sexuality. While the 16th-century seer could not have foreseen the complexities of modern life, his quatrains resonate with the ongoing transformations in societal norms, the advent of revolutionary technologies, and the shifting understanding of gender and sexual identity. This chapter delves into Nostradamus's cryptic clues, exploring their potential implications for the future of human sexuality.

The "Great Change" and the "New Loves"

In Century III, Quatrain 97, Nostradamus speaks of a "new order of the centuries" that will bring about "great inventions" and "strange enterprises." While often interpreted in political or technological contexts, some scholars suggest that this quatrain could also foreshadow significant shifts in social norms, including those related to sexuality.

The 21st century has witnessed a growing acceptance of diverse sexual orientations and gender identities. The legalisation of same-sex marriage in many countries, the increasing visibility of transgender and non-binary individuals, and the ongoing conversations about consent and sexual expression all point towards a more inclusive and open-minded approach to sexuality.

Nostradamus's prophecies, with their cryptic references to "new loves" and "unconventional unions," could be seen as hinting at these evolving social norms. While his verses lack specificity, they invite us to contemplate a future where love and intimacy are not constrained by traditional expectations or binary categories.

Virtual Intimacy and AI Companionship

The rise of virtual reality (VR) and artificial intelligence (AI) has opened up new possibilities for exploring intimacy and connection. Virtual worlds offer spaces for experimentation and self-discovery, while AI companions provide emotional support and companionship without the complexities of human relationships.

Nostradamus, in Century I, Quatrain 87, speaks of a "new engine" that will cause "great riches to change masters." While often interpreted in economic terms, this quatrain could also be seen as a reference to the transformative power of technology on our intimate lives. The "new engine" could symbolize VR and AI, which are already reshaping the landscape of human sexuality.

However, the rise of virtual intimacy and AI companionship also raises ethical concerns about the potential for addiction, isolation, and the commodification of relationships. As we navigate this uncharted territory, it is crucial to consider the impact of technology on our emotional well-being and to ensure that virtual connections complement, rather than replace, genuine human interaction.

The Fluidity of Gender and Sexual Identity

In a world where traditional gender roles are being challenged and redefined, Nostradamus's prophecies offer a glimpse into a future where gender and sexual identity are more fluid and diverse. Century IX, Quatrain 47, mentions a "great change" in the "rule of women," which could be interpreted as a prediction of greater gender equality and empowerment.

The increasing visibility of transgender and non-binary individuals is challenging binary notions of gender and sexuality, paving the way for a more inclusive and accepting society. Nostradamus's prophecies, while not explicitly mentioning these identities, could be seen as reflecting the ongoing evolution of human sexuality and the expanding spectrum of gender expression.

The Nostradamian Lens on Human Sexuality

Nostradamus's prophecies, while open to interpretation, offer a unique lens through which to view the complex and ever-evolving landscape of human sexuality. They encourage us to question traditional norms, embrace diversity, and explore new possibilities for intimacy and connection.

As we navigate the challenges and opportunities of the 21st century, Nostradamus's verses remind us that sexuality is not a static concept but a dynamic and multifaceted aspect of human experience. By fostering open-mindedness, empathy, and respect for individual choices, we can create a world where love, intimacy, and self-expression are celebrated in all their forms.

CHAPTER 59: GLOBAL RESOURCE MANAGEMENT: NOSTRADAMUS'S WARNINGS AND THE QUEST FOR SUSTAINABILITY

In the cryptic verses of Nostradamus, we find eerie premonitions of a world grappling with the scarcity and unequal distribution of natural resources. While his prophecies date back to the 16th century, they resonate with the pressing environmental challenges of the 21st century, prompting us to reflect on the potential consequences of unsustainable practices and the urgent need for global cooperation in resource management.

The "Thirsty Earth" and the "Burning Fields"

Nostradamus, in Century II, Quatrain 46, paints a bleak picture of a world plagued by drought, famine, and conflict. This quatrain, often interpreted as a prediction of environmental catastrophes, serves as a stark reminder of the finite nature of resources and the potential for their depletion to trigger social unrest and political instability.

In Century I, Quatrain 55, he speaks of a "great famine" that will return, "so great and long that they will grab roots from the trees." This chilling image could be interpreted as a warning of widespread food shortages caused by resource scarcity, soil degradation, and the impact of climate change on agricultural productivity.

The Scramble for Resources: A 21st-Century Reality

In 2024, the world is witnessing a growing competition for natural resources, such as water, oil, and rare earth minerals. The demand for these resources is driven by population growth, industrialization, and technological advancements. However, the finite nature of these resources, coupled with geopolitical tensions and unsustainable extraction practices, is creating a perfect storm of scarcity and conflict.

The ongoing water crisis in many parts of the world, the geopolitical tensions surrounding oil reserves, and the environmental devastation caused by mining rare earth minerals are all examples of the challenges we face in managing our planet's resources. Nostradamus's prophecies, while not explicitly mentioning these specific issues, can be seen as foreshadowing the potential consequences of our unsustainable practices.

Technological Solutions for Resource Scarcity

Despite the grim outlook presented by some of Nostradamus's prophecies, his verses also hint at the potential for human ingenuity to find solutions to these challenges. In Century III, Quatrain 97, he speaks of a "new order of the centuries" that will bring about "great inventions." This could be interpreted as a prediction of technological breakthroughs that will revolutionize resource management and enable us to utilize resources more efficiently and sustainably.

In recent years, we have seen significant advancements in renewable energy technologies, water purification methods, and precision agriculture techniques. These innovations offer hope for a future where we can meet the needs of a growing population without depleting the planet's resources.

Global Cooperation: A Nostradamian Imperative

Nostradamus's prophecies emphasize the interconnectedness of global events and the importance of international cooperation. In Century VI, Quatrain 21, he speaks of a "great peace" that will be achieved through the "union of nations." This could be interpreted as a call for global collaboration in addressing the challenges of resource scarcity and ensuring equitable access to essential resources for all.

In 2024, the international community is grappling with the complex issue of resource governance, as nations negotiate agreements on climate change, biodiversity conservation, and the equitable distribution of resources. Nostradamus's prophecies remind us that the fate of our planet depends on our ability to work together and find solutions that benefit all of humanity.

The Future of Resource Management: A Nostradamian Reflection

Nostradamus's prophecies, while open to interpretation, offer a unique perspective on the future of global resource management. They challenge us to confront the consequences of unsustainable practices, to embrace innovative solutions, and to prioritize cooperation over conflict.

As we navigate the 21st century, Nostradamus's verses serve as a reminder of the delicate balance between human needs and the Earth's finite resources. By heeding his warnings and embracing a more sustainable and equitable approach to resource management, we can create a future where prosperity and environmental stewardship go hand in hand.

Questions for Reflection:

1.   How do Nostradamus's prophecies about resource scarcity resonate with current environmental challenges?

2.   What are the most promising technological solutions for addressing resource scarcity?

3.   How can we foster global cooperation to ensure equitable access to resources and protect the environment

for future generations?

CHAPTER 60: THE EVOLUTION OF MUSIC AND SOUND: NOSTRADAMUS'S RESONANCE IN THE SONIC LANDSCAPE

Nostradamus, the enigmatic 16th-century seer, may not have foreseen the electric guitar, the synthesizer, or the rise of digital music production, but his cryptic verses contain intriguing hints of a future where sound and music undergo a radical transformation. This chapter delves into Nostradamus's prophecies, exploring their potential connections to the evolution of musical expression, the impact of artificial intelligence (AI) and neurotechnology on music creation and perception, and the emergence of new sonic experiences that challenge our understanding of what music can be.

The "Celestial Harmony" and the "New Instruments"

In Century IV, Quatrain 50, Nostradamus writes:

_"The heavens will sing with a new sound,

The earth will tremble with a mighty roar,

The old ways will be forgotten,

And new music will rise from the ashes._
This quatrain, with its evocative imagery of celestial music and earthly upheaval, has been interpreted as a prediction of revolutionary changes in the world of music. The "new sound" could represent the emergence of new genres, instruments, or even entirely new ways of creating and experiencing music.

In the 21st century, we are witnessing a proliferation of musical styles and instruments, from electronic music and digital synthesizers to experimental soundscapes and interactive installations. The advent of AI-powered music composition tools and neurotechnology that allows for direct brain-computer interfaces further expands the possibilities for musical expression. Nostradamus's prophecies, while not explicitly mentioning these specific technologies, could be seen as foreshadowing this sonic revolution.

The Rise of AI-Generated Music

AI is increasingly being used to compose, arrange, and even perform music. Algorithms can analyze vast amounts of musical data to identify patterns and generate new compositions that mimic the style of human composers. This raises intriguing questions about the nature of creativity and the role of technology in artistic expression.

Nostradamus, in Century I, Quatrain 87, speaks of a "new engine" that will cause "great riches to change masters." This could be interpreted as a reference to AI, which has the potential to disrupt the music industry by democratizing access to music creation tools and challenging traditional notions of authorship and ownership.

The Impact of Neurotechnology on Music Perception

Neurotechnology is also transforming the way we experience music. Researchers are developing brain-computer interfaces that allow individuals to control musical instruments with their thoughts or to experience music in entirely new ways.

Nostradamus, in Century III, Quatrain 34, speaks of a time when "the mind will be opened to the heavens." This could be interpreted as a prediction of the development of neurotechnology that enables direct interaction between the brain and music, allowing for deeper emotional engagement and potentially even therapeutic applications.

The Future of Music: A Nostradamian Perspective

Nostradamus's prophecies, while open to interpretation, offer a unique perspective on the evolving landscape of music and sound. They challenge us to envision a future where musical expression is no longer limited by traditional instruments or genres, where AI and neurotechnology expand the boundaries of creativity, and where music becomes a more immersive and personalized experience.

As we navigate this uncharted territory, Nostradamus's verses remind us of the power of music to connect, inspire, and transform. By embracing innovation, exploring new sonic frontiers, and fostering a diverse and inclusive musical landscape, we can ensure that music continues to enrich our lives and shape our cultural identities.

Questions for Reflection:

1.	How do Nostradamus's prophecies about music resonate with current trends and developments in the music industry?

2.	What are the potential implications of AI-generated music for artists, composers, and audiences?

3.	How could neurotechnology transform the way we experience and interact with music?

CHAPTER 61:
THE FUTURE OF CHILDHOOD AND EDUCATION: A NOSTRADAMIAN LENS ON THE NEXT GENERATION

In the cryptic verses of Nostradamus, we find intriguing allusions to the ever-evolving nature of childhood and education. While his 16th-century perspective could not have fully envisioned the digital age and its impact on young minds, his prophecies resonate with contemporary concerns about child development, the role of technology in learning, and the shifting landscape of educational systems.

"The Young Lions" and the "New Learning"

Nostradamus, in Century III, Quatrain 97, speaks of a "new order of the centuries" that will bring about "great inventions" and "strange enterprises." While often interpreted in broader societal contexts, this quatrain could also foreshadow a transformation in education, where new technologies and pedagogies emerge to shape the minds of the next generation.

In Century I, Quatrain 50, Nostradamus mentions "young lions" who will "roar with a new voice." This could be interpreted as a metaphor for a generation of children who grow up in a world vastly different from that of their parents, empowered by technology and eager to challenge established norms.

The Impact of Technology on Childhood Experiences

In the 21st century, children are immersed in a digital world from a young age. Smartphones, tablets, and computers have become ubiquitous, offering access to vast amounts of information and entertainment. While technology can be a powerful tool for learning and creativity, it also raises concerns about screen time addiction, cyberbullying, and the erosion of traditional social skills.

Nostradamus, in Century VI, Quatrain 97, warns of a "great deception" that will "corrupt the minds of the young." This could be interpreted as a cautionary tale about the potential negative effects of technology on child development, such as the spread of misinformation, the normalization of violence in video games, and the blurring of boundaries between the real and virtual worlds.

However, Nostradamus also hints at the positive potential of technology to empower and educate young people. In Century X, Quatrain 72, he speaks of a "new knowledge" that will be "revealed to the world." This could be seen as a reference to the vast educational resources available online and the potential for technology to democratize access to learning.

Changing Educational Paradigms

The traditional model of education, with its emphasis on rote memorization and standardized testing, is increasingly being challenged by alternative approaches that emphasize creativity, critical thinking, and collaboration. The rise of online learning platforms, personalized learning plans, and project-based learning are all examples of this shift towards a more student-cantered and adaptable educational model.

Nostradamus's prophecies, while not explicitly mentioning

these specific changes, could be seen as foreshadowing the evolution of educational systems. The "new learning" mentioned in his verses could represent the emergence of new pedagogical approaches that harness the power of technology and cater to the diverse needs and interests of learners.

The Nostradamian Perspective on the Future of Education

Nostradamus's prophecies, while open to interpretation, offer a unique lens through which to view the challenges and opportunities facing education in the 21st century. They remind us of the importance of adapting to a rapidly changing world, embracing new technologies, and prioritizing the well-being and development of young people.

As we navigate this uncharted territory, Nostradamus's verses encourage us to question traditional assumptions about education and to explore innovative approaches that prepare children for a future that is increasingly complex and interconnected.

Questions for Reflection:

1.	How do Nostradamus's prophecies about childhood and education resonate with current trends and challenges in the field?

2.	What are the potential benefits and risks of technology in education?

3.	How can we create educational systems that empower children to thrive in the 21st century?

By engaging in thoughtful dialogue, embracing new ideas, and prioritizing the needs of children, we can create a future where education is not only a means to an end but a transformative journey of self-discovery and lifelong learning.

CHAPTER 62: ADVANCEMENTS IN NANOTECHNOLOGY: NOSTRADAMUS'S VISION OF THE INVISIBLE WORLD

Nostradamus, a visionary seer of the 16th century, lived in a world where the concept of manipulating matter at the atomic level was unimaginable. Yet, some interpretations of his cryptic quatrains suggest that he may have glimpsed a future where humanity harnesses the power of nanotechnology to reshape the world around us. This chapter delves into Nostradamus's enigmatic prophecies, exploring their potential connections to advancements in nanotechnology, the diverse applications of this transformative technology, and the ethical considerations that arise as we venture into the realm of the infinitesimally small.

The "Hidden Arts" and the "Invisible World"

In Century I, Quatrain 63, Nostradamus writes:

_The hidden arts will come to light,

The world will be renewed by a new man,

Who will know the secrets of the stars,

And will change the course of human destiny._
This quatrain, with its reference to "hidden arts," has been interpreted by some as a prediction of the emergence of nanotechnology, a field that operates at the nanoscale, manipulating matter at the atomic and molecular level. The "new man" could represent a future generation of scientists and engineers who harness this technology to create new materials, medicines, and devices with unprecedented capabilities.

In Century II, Quatrain 41, Nostradamus speaks of a "new creature" that will emerge from the earth, causing "great terror and confusion." This could be interpreted as a reference to the potential risks and unintended consequences of nanotechnology, such as the creation of self-replicating nanobots or the accidental release of nanoparticles into the environment.

Nanotechnology in 2024: A Burgeoning Field

As of 2024, nanotechnology is a rapidly growing field with applications in diverse industries, including medicine, electronics, energy, and materials science. Nanoparticles are being used to deliver drugs directly to cancer cells, enhance the efficiency of solar panels, and create stronger and lighter materials for construction and manufacturing.

Nostradamus's prophecies, while not explicitly mentioning nanotechnology, could be seen as foreshadowing these developments. The "great inventions" and "strange enterprises" he describes could be interpreted as references to the transformative potential of nanotechnology to reshape our world.

The Potential of Nanotechnology: A Double-Edged Sword

The promise of nanotechnology is immense. It has the potential to revolutionize medicine by enabling targeted drug delivery, regenerative therapies, and even the creation of artificial organs. In manufacturing, nanotechnology could lead to the development of new materials with unprecedented properties, such as self-healing materials and ultra-strong composites. In environmental science, nanoparticles could be used to clean up pollution, remediate contaminated sites, and even capture carbon dioxide from the atmosphere.

However, the potential of nanotechnology also comes with risks. The long-term health and environmental effects of nanoparticles are not yet fully understood, and there are concerns about the potential for misuse of this technology for military or malicious purposes.

Ethical Considerations and the Path Forward

As we embrace the potential of nanotechnology, it is crucial to consider the ethical implications of this powerful tool. How do we ensure that nanotechnology is used for the benefit of humanity, rather than for harm? How do we balance the pursuit of progress with the need to protect human health and the environment?

Nostradamus's prophecies, with their warnings of "great terror and confusion," serve as a reminder of the potential dangers of unchecked technological advancement. As we venture into the world of nanotechnology, we must proceed with caution, guided by ethical principles and a commitment to the responsible use of this transformative technology.

The Nostradamian Perspective on Nanotechnology

Nostradamus's prophecies, while open to interpretation, offer a unique perspective on the future of nanotechnology. They challenge us to envision a world where the manipulation of matter at the atomic level becomes commonplace, where new materials and technologies revolutionize our lives, and where the boundaries between the natural and the artificial become increasingly blurred.

As we navigate this uncharted territory, Nostradamus's verses remind us of the importance of foresight, ethical responsibility, and a commitment to the well-being of both humanity and the planet. By embracing nanotechnology with wisdom and caution, we can harness its potential to create a more sustainable, equitable, and prosperous future for all.

CHAPTER 63: THE EVOLUTION OF FASHION AND BODY MODIFICATION: NOSTRADAMUS'S GLIMPSE INTO A FUTURE OF SELF-EXPRESSION

Nostradamus, the enigmatic 16th-century seer, may not have envisioned haute couture or cyberpunk aesthetics, but his quatrains offer intriguing hints of a future where fashion and body modification undergo radical transformations. This chapter delves into Nostradamus's prophecies, exploring their potential connections to the evolving landscape of self-expression, the rise of innovative materials and technologies, and the increasing acceptance of extreme body modifications.

The "Clothed in Colors" and the "Changing Skin"

In Century I, Quatrain 42, Nostradamus writes:

_The great city will be besieged and assaulted,
Its inhabitants will be clothed in colors,

A new fashion will emerge from the East,
And the old ways will be forgotten._
This quatrain, while often interpreted as a prediction of war and social upheaval, could also be seen as a metaphor for the changing landscape of fashion. The "clothed in colors" could refer to a future where self-expression through clothing becomes more vibrant and diverse, while the "new fashion from the East" could allude to the increasing influence of Asian cultures on global fashion trends.

In Century II, Quatrain 65, Nostradamus speaks of "a changing skin" that will "reveal the secrets of the heart." This enigmatic phrase could be interpreted as a reference to body modification, where individuals alter their physical appearance to express their identity, beliefs, or values. Tattoos, piercings, and even implants are becoming increasingly mainstream, blurring the lines between the natural and the artificial.

Innovative Materials and Smart Clothing

In the 21st century, the fashion industry is embracing technological innovation, with the development of smart fabrics, 3D-printed clothing, and wearable technology that integrates seamlessly with our bodies. These advancements are revolutionizing the way we think about clothing, transforming it from a mere covering into a tool for communication, self-expression, and even health monitoring.

Nostradamus, in Century III, Quatrain 97, speaks of a "new order of the centuries" that will bring about "great inventions." This could be interpreted as a foreshadowing of the rise of wearable technology and the integration of electronics into our clothing, creating a new paradigm of fashion that blends the physical and the digital.

The Acceptance of Extreme Body Modification

As technology advances, the possibilities for body modification become increasingly limitless. From biohacking to genetic engineering, individuals are pushing the boundaries of what it means to be human, challenging traditional notions of beauty and identity.

Nostradamus, in Century VIII, Quatrain 55, mentions "unnatural offspring" that will "rise from the depths." This could be interpreted as a reference to individuals who undergo extreme body modifications, transforming themselves into beings that defy conventional norms.

The Rise of Body Positivity and Self-Acceptance

While extreme body modifications may seem shocking to some, they are part of a broader movement towards body positivity and self-acceptance. In a world where unrealistic beauty standards are constantly bombarded upon us, body modification can be a way for individuals to reclaim their bodies and express their individuality.

Nostradamus's prophecies, while open to interpretation, offer a unique perspective on the evolving landscape of fashion and body modification. They challenge us to question our assumptions about beauty, identity, and self-expression, and to embrace the diversity and creativity of human experience.

As we navigate the complexities of the 21st century, Nostradamus's verses remind us that fashion is not merely a superficial concern, but a reflection of our values, aspirations, and cultural identities. By embracing innovation, celebrating diversity, and challenging societal norms, we can create a future where fashion and body modification are tools for empowerment, self-discovery, and creative expression.

Questions for Reflection:

1. How do Nostradamus's prophecies about fashion and body modification resonate with current trends and debates?

2. What are the potential benefits and risks of technological advancements in fashion and body modification?

3. How can we create a society that embraces diversity in appearance and self-expression?

CHAPTER 64: THE FUTURE OF SLEEP AND DREAMS: NOSTRADAMUS'S GLIMPSE INTO THE NOCTURNAL REALM

The realm of sleep and dreams, a mysterious and elusive domain of human experience, has long captured the imagination of poets, philosophers, and scientists alike. Nostradamus, with his cryptic verses and enigmatic imagery, offers a unique perspective on this elusive realm, hinting at a future where our understanding and control over sleep and dreams may undergo a profound transformation.

The "Great Slumber" and the "Hidden Messages"

In Century I, Quatrain 55, Nostradamus warns of a "great famine" that will bring "great sorrow" to the world. While traditionally interpreted as a prophecy of widespread hunger, this quatrain could also be seen as a metaphor for a collective sleep deprivation crisis. In our modern society, characterized by 24/7 connectivity and ever-increasing demands on our time and attention, sleep deprivation is a growing concern. Could Nostradamus's prophecy be a warning about the potential consequences of neglecting our need for rest and rejuvenation?

In Century II, Quatrain 43, he speaks of "hidden messages" that will be "revealed in dreams." This quatrain hints at the possibility that dreams may hold deeper meaning and significance than we currently understand. Throughout history, dreams have been viewed as portals to the subconscious, sources of divine inspiration, or even premonitions of future events.

As science delves deeper into the mysteries of sleep and dreams, we may discover new ways to interpret and harness the power of our nocturnal visions. Research on lucid dreaming, for example, suggests that individuals can learn to become aware of their dreams and even control their content, opening up new possibilities for self-discovery, creativity, and healing.

Scientific Breakthroughs in Sleep Research

In the 21st century, scientific research is shedding new light on the intricate mechanisms of sleep and its impact on our physical and mental health. Studies have linked sleep deprivation to a range of health problems, including obesity, heart disease, and cognitive decline. Conversely, adequate sleep has been shown to boost immunity, improve memory, and enhance overall well-being.

Nostradamus, in Century VIII, Quatrain 35, mentions a "celestial fire" that will "descend from the heavens" and "bring about great changes." This could be interpreted as a metaphor for a scientific breakthrough in sleep research, perhaps the discovery of new therapies or technologies that can optimize sleep patterns, treat sleep disorders, and unlock the full potential of our dreams.

Shared Dreams and the Collective Unconscious

The concept of shared or collective dreams has fascinated philosophers and psychologists for centuries. Carl Jung, the Swiss psychiatrist, proposed the existence of a "collective unconscious," a shared reservoir of archetypes and symbols that manifest in our dreams.

Nostradamus's prophecies, with their recurring imagery of celestial events and mythological figures, could be seen as tapping into this collective unconscious. His verses may not predict specific dreams but rather allude to universal themes and archetypes that resonate across cultures and time periods. In the digital age, the idea of shared dreams has taken on a new dimension with the emergence of technologies that allow individuals to record and share their dreams online. Could this lead to a deeper understanding of the collective unconscious and its potential impact on human society?

The Future of Sleep and Dreams: A Nostradamian Perspective

Nostradamus's prophecies, while open to interpretation, offer a unique perspective on the future of sleep and dreams. They challenge us to reconsider the role of sleep in our lives, to explore the hidden meanings of our dreams, and to embrace the potential of technology to unlock the mysteries of the nocturnal realm.

As we navigate the 21st century, Nostradamus's verses remind us of the importance of rest, rejuvenation, and the power of the subconscious mind. By prioritizing sleep, exploring our dreams, and embracing new technologies that enhance our understanding of the sleeping brain, we can tap into the full potential of our consciousness and create a more harmonious and fulfilling life.

Questions for Reflection:

1.   How do Nostradamus's prophecies about sleep and dreams resonate with current scientific research and cultural trends?

2.   What are the potential implications of shared dreams and the collective unconscious for human society?

3.   How can we leverage technology to improve sleep quality and unlock the transformative power of our dreams?

CHAPTER 65: NEW FORMS OF GOVERNMENT AND SOCIAL ORGANIZATION: NOSTRADAMUS'S VISION OF THE FUTURE STATE

The 16th-century prophecies of Nostradamus, shrouded in mystery and symbolism, have captivated audiences for centuries. While often interpreted as foretelling dramatic events, a closer examination of his quatrains reveals intriguing allusions to potential transformations in government and social organization. This chapter delves into these predictions, exploring their relevance to contemporary discussions about decentralized autonomous organizations (DAOs), artificial intelligence (AI)-assisted governance, and the ongoing evolution of political systems.

The "New Order" and the "Fall of the Mighty"

In Century III, Quatrain 97, Nostradamus writes:

_The new order of the centuries will be renewed,
It will return to its high, heroic, and primeval state,
The great monarch will be restored by the favour of God,
The people will be happy and the world at peace._

This quatrain, while open to multiple interpretations, hints at a significant shift in the political landscape. Some scholars suggest it foretells the decline of traditional hierarchical structures and the emergence of new forms of governance characterized by greater participation and decentralization.

The "fall of the mighty" could be interpreted as the demise of centralized authorities and the rise of more democratic and inclusive systems. This aligns with the growing interest in decentralized autonomous organizations (DAOs), which are governed by code and consensus rather than by hierarchical structures.

The Rise of DAOs: A New Paradigm of Governance

DAOs, powered by blockchain technology, offer a radical new approach to organizational governance. They are decentralized, transparent, and community-driven, allowing for collective decision-making and resource allocation without the need for central authorities. While still in their infancy, DAOs have the potential to disrupt traditional models of governance and empower individuals to participate more directly in decision-making processes.

Nostradamus's prophecies, while not explicitly mentioning DAOs, resonate with the principles of decentralization and community-driven governance. In Century I, Quatrain 50, he speaks of a time when "the great will fall from their high places, and the humble will be exalted." This could be interpreted as a prediction of the empowerment of individuals and communities through decentralized structures like DAOs.

AI-Assisted Governance: A Nostradamian Vision?

Artificial intelligence (AI) is rapidly transforming various aspects of society, from healthcare and transportation to finance and entertainment. In the realm of governance, AI has the potential to streamline decision-making, enhance transparency, and improve efficiency.

Nostradamus's prophecies, with their cryptic references to "new engines" and "hidden arts," could be seen as foreshadowing the use of AI in governance. The "new sage with a lone brain," mentioned in Century II, Quatrain 52,could represent an AI system that analyses vast amounts of data and provides insights to policymakers, enabling more informed and evidence-based decision-making.

However, the use of AI in governance also raises ethical concerns about bias, accountability, and the potential for misuse. Nostradamus's prophecies serve as a reminder of the importance of human oversight and ethical considerations in the development and deployment of AI systems.

The Future of Governance: A Nostradamian Reflection

Nostradamus's prophecies, while open to interpretation, offer a unique lens through which to view the evolving landscape of governance. They challenge us to envision a future where new technologies and social movements reshape traditional power structures and empower individuals to participate more directly in decision-making processes.

As we navigate the complexities of the 21st century, Nostradamus's verses remind us that the future of governance is not predetermined. It is a dynamic and ongoing process that requires continuous innovation, adaptation, and a commitment to democratic values. By embracing new technologies, fostering transparency, and empowering individuals, we can create a more just, equitable, and sustainable world for all.

CHAPTER 66: THE TRANSFORMATION OF TIME PERCEPTION: NOSTRADAMUS'S GLIMPSE INTO THE FOURTH DIMENSION

Time, an ever-present yet enigmatic concept, has perplexed philosophers and scientists for millennia. Nostradamus, with his cryptic verses and enigmatic imagery, offers a unique perspective on the nature of time and its potential for transformation. While rooted in the 16th century, his prophecies hint at a future where our perception and experience of time may be radically altered, raising profound questions about the nature of reality, the impact of technology on our temporal awareness, and the potential for new dimensions of consciousness.

The "Great Cycle" and the "New Age"

Nostradamus, in Century II, Quatrain 46, writes of a "great cycle of the centuries renewed." This cyclical view of time, common in ancient cultures, suggests that history repeats itself in patterns, with events and eras mirroring each other across vast stretches of time. In the context of 2024, this quatrain could be interpreted as a warning of impending upheaval and a return to past conflicts.

However, other interpretations suggest a more optimistic outlook, pointing towards a "new age" marked by spiritual awakening and societal transformation. This aligns with the concept of the "Age of Aquarius," a period of enlightenment and progressive change that some astrologers believe we are currently entering. Could Nostradamus's prophecy be hinting at a shift in consciousness that alters our perception of time and our place in the grand scheme of things?

The Relativity of Time: A Scientific Perspective

In the 20th century, Einstein's theory of relativity revolutionized our understanding of time, revealing its interconnectedness with space and its dependence on the observer's frame of reference. This ground-breaking theory has profound implications for our perception of time, suggesting that it is not a fixed and universal constant but rather a fluid and subjective experience.

Nostradamus, with his cryptic references to "celestial spheres" and "the movement of the stars," could be seen as intuitively grasping the relativity of time. His prophecies, while not scientifically precise, resonate with the notion that time is not a linear progression but a multi-dimensional tapestry woven with threads of past, present, and future.

Technology and the Manipulation of Time

In the 21st century, technology is increasingly blurring the lines between the past, present, and future. Social media platforms allow us to relive past experiences and connect with friends and family across different time zones. Virtual reality technology immerses us in simulated environments, creating a sense of timelessness and detachment from the present moment. And the rapid pace of technological change creates a sense of accelerated time, where the future seems to arrive ever faster.

Nostradamus, in Century III, Quatrain 97, speaks of a "new order of the centuries" that will bring about "great inventions." This could be interpreted as a prediction of technologies that further manipulate our perception of time, such as time dilation devices or virtual reality simulations that alter our sense of temporal flow.

The Future of Time: A Nostradamian Reflection

Nostradamus's prophecies, while open to interpretation, offer a unique perspective on the nature of time and its potential for transformation. They challenge us to question our assumptions about the linear progression of time, to explore the subjective nature of our temporal experiences, and to consider the impact of technology on our perception of the past, present, and future.

As we navigate the 21st century, Nostradamus's verses remind us that time is not a rigid construct but a fluid and dynamic force. By embracing new technologies, exploring alternative perspectives on time, and cultivating mindfulness of the present moment, we can unlock new dimensions of experience and create a more meaningful and fulfilling life.

Questions for Reflection:

1. How do Nostradamus's prophecies about time resonate with current scientific understanding and technological advancements?

2. What are the potential implications of altered time perception for individuals and society?

3. How can we harness technology to enhance our temporal awareness and live more fulfilling lives?

CHAPTER 67:
THE FUTURE OF HUMAN MEMORY: NOSTRADAMUS'S VISIONS OF REMEMBRANCE AND FORGETTING

The human mind, a complex labyrinth of memories, thoughts, and emotions, has long fascinated philosophers, scientists, and seers alike. Nostradamus, with his cryptic verses and enigmatic imagery, offers a unique perspective on the future of human memory, hinting at both the potential for enhancement and the perils of manipulation. As we navigate the 21st century, a time of rapid technological advancements and burgeoning neuroscientific discoveries, Nostradamus's prophecies invite us to contemplate the evolving nature of memory, the impact of technology on our recollections, and the ethical implications of manipulating our past experiences.

The "Hidden Book" and the "New Memory"

In Century II, Quatrain 28, Nostradamus writes:

_"The lost book of the Seven Seals will be found,

Revealing secrets hidden for a thousand years,
A new memory will arise from the ashes of the old,
And humanity will be forever changed._

This quatrain, steeped in biblical imagery, has been interpreted as a prediction of the discovery of lost knowledge or the emergence of a new paradigm of understanding. In the context of memory, this could refer to breakthroughs in neuroscience that unlock the secrets of how memories are formed, stored, and retrieved.

The "new memory" mentioned in the quatrain could symbolize the advent of technologies that augment or even replace our biological memory. In the 21st century, researchers are exploring the potential of brain-computer interfaces, memory implants, and even digital consciousness to enhance memory capacity and preserve our experiences for posterity.

The Power of Technology: Enhancing and Erasing Memories

Technology has already revolutionized the way we store and access memories. From photographs and videos to social media posts and cloud storage, we have an unprecedented ability to document and share our lives. However, this reliance on external memory aids also raises questions about the authenticity and reliability of our memories.

Nostradamus, in Century IV, Quatrain 92, writes of a time when "the past will be rewritten" and "truth will be obscured." This could be interpreted as a warning about the potential for technology to manipulate our memories, creating false narratives or erasing inconvenient truths.

The ethical implications of memory manipulation are profound. Should we have the right to erase traumatic memories or alter our past experiences? How do we ensure the accuracy and integrity of historical records in the digital age? These questions raise complex issues about personal identity, autonomy, and the nature of truth itself.

Nostradamus's Vision of the Future of Memory

Nostradamus's prophecies, while open to interpretation, offer a thought-provoking perspective on the future of human memory. They challenge us to consider the potential benefits and risks of technological advancements, the ethical implications of memory manipulation, and the importance of preserving our collective past.

As we navigate the complexities of the 21st century, Nostradamus's verses remind us that memory is not a static entity but a dynamic and malleable construct. By embracing new technologies with caution, fostering critical thinking, and valuing the diversity of human experience, we can create a future where memory serves as a bridge between the past and the present, enriching our lives and shaping our collective future.

Questions for Reflection:

1.	How do Nostradamus's prophecies about memory resonate with current developments in neuroscience and technology?

2.	What are the potential benefits and risks of enhancing or manipulating human memory?

3.	How can we ensure that the pursuit of technological advancement does not compromise our ethical values and the integrity of our memories?

CHAPTER 68: EXTRA-TERRESTRIAL CONTACT AND ITS AFTERMATH: NOSTRADAMUS'S VISIONS OF A COSMIC ENCOUNTER

Nostradamus's prophetic verses, steeped in celestial imagery and apocalyptic visions, have long fuelled speculation about potential contact with extra-terrestrial life. While the 16th-century seer could not have imagined the scientific advancements that have allowed us to explore the cosmos, his enigmatic quatrains resonate with contemporary discussions about the possibility of alien civilizations and the potential impact of such an encounter on humanity.

The "Celestial Chariots" and the "Starry Messengers"

Nostradamus, in Century II, Quatrain 46, writes of a time when "the great cycle of the centuries renewed, it will rain blood, milk, famine, war and disease." While this quatrain is often interpreted as a prediction of global upheaval, some scholars believe that it could also be seen as a foreshadowing of a close encounter with extra-terrestrial life. The "blood" and "fire" mentioned in the verse could symbolize the chaos and destruction that might accompany such an event, while the "milk" could represent the potential for knowledge and enlightenment that could be gained from contact with a more advanced civilization.

In Century VI, Quatrain 97, Nostradamus speaks of a "new flame" that will accompany a "sudden lightning war." This quatrain has been interpreted by some as a prediction of a conflict involving extra-terrestrial beings, potentially triggered by a misunderstanding or a clash of cultures. The "new flame" could represent advanced alien technology, while the "lightning war" could refer to a swift and devastating conflict.

First Contact Scenarios: Hope, Fear, and Uncertainty

The prospect of encountering extra-terrestrial life has long been a source of both fascination and trepidation. Scientists, philosophers and science fiction writers have explored a wide range of potential scenarios, from peaceful cultural exchange to hostile invasion.

In the 21st century, the search for extra-terrestrial intelligence (SETI) has intensified, with radio telescopes scanning the skies for signals from distant civilizations. While no definitive evidence of extra-terrestrial life has yet been found, the possibility remains tantalizingly open.

Nostradamus's prophecies, with their cryptic references to "celestial chariots" and "starry messengers," offer a unique perspective on the potential impact of first contact. His verses suggest that such an encounter could be both transformative and disruptive, challenging our understanding of the universe and our place within it.

The Impact on Human Society and Belief Systems

The discovery of extra-terrestrial life would undoubtedly have a profound impact on human society. It would challenge our most fundamental beliefs about our place in the universe, the nature of life, and the possibility of intelligent life beyond

Earth.

Nostradamus's prophecies hint at both the positive and negative potential of such a discovery. In Century X, Quatrain 72,he speaks of a "new king" who will "rise from the East" and "bring about great changes." This could be interpreted as a prediction of a new world order that emerges in response to contact with extra-terrestrial life, perhaps leading to greater global cooperation and a renewed sense of shared humanity.

However, other quatrains warn of potential conflict and upheaval. In Century III, Quatrain 64, Nostradamus speaks of a "great earthquake" that will "change the course of the world." This could be seen as a metaphor for the seismic shift in human consciousness that would likely occur in the wake of contact with an alien civilization.

The Nostradamian Perspective on Extra-terrestrial Contact

Nostradamus's prophecies, while open to interpretation, offer a unique lens through which to view the possibility of extra-terrestrial contact. They challenge us to consider the potential consequences of such an encounter, both positive and negative, and to reflect on our own place in the cosmos.

As we continue our exploration of the universe, Nostradamus's verses remind us that we are not alone. Whether we encounter friendly or hostile aliens, or perhaps no aliens at all, the search for extra-terrestrial life is a testament to the enduring human spirit of curiosity and exploration.

CHAPTER 69: THE EVOLUTION OF HUMAN EMPATHY AND COMPASSION: A NOSTRADAMIAN REFLECTION ON OUR SHARED HUMANITY

While Nostradamus is often associated with prophecies of doom and gloom, his cryptic verses also contain hints of hope, suggesting the potential for humanity to evolve towards greater empathy and compassion. As we navigate the complexities of the 21st century, with its technological advancements, social upheavals, and environmental challenges, Nostradamus's prophecies invite us to reflect on the nature of empathy, the role of technology in fostering connection, and the possibility of a more compassionate future.

The "Great Compassion" and the "Universal Brotherhood"

In Century X, Quatrain 74, Nostradamus writes:

_The great man will be struck down in the day by a thunderbolt,

An evil deed foretold by the bearer of a petition,
According to the prediction another falls at night-time,
Conflict at Reims, London, and a pestilence in Tuscany._
While seemingly focused on political turmoil, this quatrain has been interpreted by some as a foreshadowing of a global shift in consciousness towards greater empathy and compassion. The "great man" could represent the old paradigms of individualism and competition, while the "thunderbolt" could symbolize a catalyst for change, such as a global crisis or a technological breakthrough.

In Century II, Quatrain 29, Nostradamus speaks of a "new law" that will "occupy the great world," bringing about "peace and harmony." This could be interpreted as a prediction of a global movement towards greater understanding and cooperation, driven by a shared sense of humanity and compassion for others.

The Digital Age: A Double-Edged Sword for Empathy

The rise of digital technology has transformed the way we connect with each other, enabling us to share stories, experiences, and emotions across vast distances. Social media platforms, online forums, and virtual communities have created spaces for empathy and solidarity, fostering a sense of interconnectedness and global citizenship.

However, technology can also be a double-edged sword for empathy. The constant exposure to violence and suffering in the news and social media can lead to compassion fatigue and desensitization. The anonymity and distance of online interactions can also make it easier to engage in harmful behaviours like cyberbullying and hate speech.

Nostradamus, in Century III, Quatrain 81, warns of a time when "the written word will be so obfuscated, that no one will be able to understand it at all." This could be interpreted as a cautionary tale about the potential for technology to distort communication and hinder genuine emotional connection.

Cultivating Empathy in a Changing World

In a world facing complex challenges such as climate change, social inequality, and political polarization, the need for empathy and compassion is more urgent than ever. How can we foster a more empathetic society in the face of these daunting challenges?

Nostradamus's prophecies, while not offering concrete solutions, remind us of the importance of cultivating empathy through education, dialogue, and shared experiences. By learning about different cultures, perspectives, and worldviews, we can expand our capacity for understanding and compassion.

The practice of mindfulness, meditation, and other contemplative practices can also help us to develop greater self-awareness and emotional regulation, which are essential for building empathy. By learning to observe our own thoughts and feelings without judgment, we can cultivate a greater capacity for understanding and compassion towards others.

A Nostradamian Vision for a More Compassionate Future

Nostradamus's prophecies, while often shrouded in mystery, offer a hopeful vision of a future where empathy and compassion prevail. They encourage us to strive for a world where we see ourselves in others, where we prioritize connection over conflict, and where we work together to create a more just and equitable society.

The path towards this more compassionate future is not without its challenges. We must confront the forces of division and hatred that seek to undermine our shared humanity. We must also harness the power of technology to bridge divides, foster understanding, and amplify voices of compassion and hope.

As we navigate the 21st century, Nostradamus's prophecies serve as a reminder of our interconnectedness and the potential for human kindness to transcend boundaries of culture, race, and religion. By embracing empathy as a guiding principle, we can create a world where compassion is not just a lofty ideal, but a lived reality.

CHAPTER 70: REDEFINING DEATH AND THE AFTERLIFE: NOSTRADAMUS'S GLIMPSE INTO THE ETERNAL MYSTERY

In the enigmatic verses of Nostradamus, we encounter cryptic allusions to the profound mysteries of death and the afterlife. While rooted in the spiritual and philosophical traditions of his time, these prophecies resonate with contemporary inquiries into the nature of consciousness, the possibility of life after death, and the evolving cultural and religious perspectives on this eternal enigma.

The "Great Crossing" and the "Invisible World"

Nostradamus, in Century I, Quatrain 14, speaks of a "great crossing" that will lead to "a new world." This quatrain, often interpreted as a prediction of physical journeys or migrations, could also be seen as a metaphor for the transition from life to death. The "new world" could represent the afterlife, a realm that has captivated human imagination and sparked countless religious and philosophical inquiries.

In Century II, Quatrain 51, Nostradamus mentions a "hidden world" that will be "revealed to the chosen few." This could be interpreted as a reference to near-death experiences (NDEs), where individuals report glimpses of an afterlife realm before returning to life. In recent years, scientific research has explored the phenomenon of NDEs, seeking to understand the neurobiological processes involved and the potential implications for our understanding of consciousness.

Scientific Inquiry into the Afterlife

While the concept of an afterlife remains a matter of faith for many, science is increasingly exploring the possibility of consciousness surviving bodily death. Research in fields such as quantum physics, neuroscience, and parapsychology is shedding new light on the nature of consciousness and its potential to exist independently of the physical body.

Nostradamus's prophecies, while not providing scientific evidence, could be seen as inspiring a deeper exploration of the mysteries of consciousness and the possibility of life after death. His verses, with their references to "souls" and "spirits," resonate with the enduring human quest for understanding the nature of our existence beyond the physical realm.

Changing Cultural and Religious Perspectives

The concept of the afterlife has been a central tenet of many religions and spiritual traditions throughout history. However, in the 21st century, we are witnessing a growing diversity of beliefs about what happens after death. Secularism, atheism, and agnostic viewpoints are becoming more prevalent, while traditional religious beliefs are being reinterpreted and reimagined.

Nostradamus's prophecies, while rooted in the Christian worldview of his time, can be seen as transcending specific religious dogmas. His verses speak to universal human concerns about mortality, the meaning of life, and the possibility of an afterlife.

The "End of Times" and the "New Beginning"

In Century X, Quatrain 72, Nostradamus writes:

_The blood of the just will be demanded of London,
Burnt up in the fire of '66:

The ancient Lady will fall from her high place,
Several of the same sect will be killed._
This quatrain, often interpreted as a prediction of a catastrophic event in London, could also be seen as a metaphor for the end of an era and the beginning of a new one. The "ancient Lady" could represent traditional beliefs and institutions that are being challenged, while the "new sect" could symbolize the emergence of new spiritual or philosophical movements.

Nostradamus's prophecies, with their apocalyptic imagery and references to rebirth, invite us to contemplate the cyclical nature of life and death. They remind us that endings are also beginnings, and that even in the face of loss and destruction, there is always the possibility of renewal and transformation.

The Nostradamian Perspective on Death and the Afterlife

Nostradamus's prophecies, while open to interpretation, offer a unique perspective on the perennial human quest for understanding death and the afterlife. They challenge us to question our assumptions, explore new possibilities, and embrace the mysteries that lie beyond our current understanding.

As we navigate the complexities of the 21st century, Nostradamus's verses remind us that death is not the end, but rather a transition to another realm of existence. Whether we believe in heaven, reincarnation, or the continuation of consciousness in another form, the exploration of the afterlife remains a fundamental aspect of the human experience.

Questions for Reflection:

1.	How do Nostradamus's prophecies about death and the afterlife resonate with your own beliefs and experiences?

2.	What are the potential implications of scientific research into consciousness and near-death experiences for our understanding of the afterlife?

3.	How do you envision the future of human spirituality and beliefs about the afterlife?

CHAPTER 71: THE FUTURE OF HUMAN HABITATS: NOSTRADAMUS'S VISION OF DWELLING PLACES AND THE IMPACT OF CHANGE

As the global population continues to grow and climate change accelerates, the future of human habitats becomes a pressing concern. Nostradamus, the enigmatic 16th-century seer, may not have explicitly envisioned skyscrapers or eco-friendly homes, but his cryptic verses offer intriguing glimpses into a future where our living spaces undergo profound transformations. This chapter delves into Nostradamus's prophecies, exploring their relevance to contemporary discussions about sustainable architecture, adaptable housing, and the impact of environmental change on human settlements.

The "Great City" and the "New Babylon"

In Century II, Quatrain 52, Nostradamus speaks of a "great city" that will be "thoroughly burned." While often interpreted as a prediction of destruction, this quatrain could also be seen as a warning about the vulnerability of traditional urban environments to natural disasters and climate change. The "great city" could symbolize any major metropolis grappling with overcrowding, pollution, and inadequate infrastructure.

In contrast, Nostradamus also mentions a "new city" that will rise from the ashes. This could be interpreted as a vision of a more resilient and sustainable urban environment, designed to withstand the challenges of the 21st century. This interpretation aligns with the growing movement towards green architecture and eco-friendly urban planning, which seek to minimize the environmental impact of human settlements.

Innovative Housing Solutions: A Nostradamian Perspective

Nostradamus's prophecies, while often shrouded in mystery, could be seen as foreshadowing the emergence of innovative housing solutions. In Century III, Quatrain 97, he speaks of a "new order of the centuries" that will bring about "great inventions." This could be interpreted as a reference to the development of new building materials, construction techniques, and architectural designs that prioritize sustainability, adaptability, and resilience.

In the 21st century, we are witnessing a surge in innovation in the field of housing. From 3D-printed homes to modular construction, architects and engineers are exploring new ways to create affordable, efficient, and environmentally friendly living spaces. These innovations could offer solutions to the challenges of rapid urbanization, housing shortages, and climate change-induced displacement.

Climate Change and the Future of Human Settlements

As the effects of climate change become increasingly evident, the vulnerability of human settlements to extreme weather events, rising sea levels, and resource scarcity is becoming more apparent. Nostradamus's prophecies, with their warnings of "floods," "fire," and "great upheavals," serve as stark reminders of the need to adapt our habitats to a changing environment.

In Century I, Quatrain 69, Nostradamus writes:

The dry earth will grow more parched, and there will be great floods when it is seen.

This quatrain could be interpreted as a prediction of both drought and floods, two extreme weather events that are already causing significant disruption to human settlements around the world. The need for climate-resilient infrastructure and adaptive housing solutions has never been more urgent.

The Nostradamian Challenge: Building a Sustainable Future

Nostradamus's prophecies, while open to interpretation, offer a unique lens through which to view the future of human habitats. They challenge us to envision a world where our living spaces are not only aesthetically pleasing but also sustainable, resilient, and adaptable to the challenges of the 21st century.

As we grapple with the complex interplay of social, economic, and environmental factors that shape our built environment, Nostradamus's verses remind us of the importance of foresight, innovation, and a deep respect for the natural world. By embracing sustainable practices, investing in resilient infrastructure, and fostering a culture of environmental stewardship, we can create a future where human habitats thrive in harmony with the planet.

Questions for Reflection:

1.	How do Nostradamus's prophecies about human habitats resonate with contemporary concerns about climate change and urbanization?

2.	What are the most promising innovations in sustainable architecture and housing?

3.	How can we create cities and communities that are resilient to the challenges of the 21st century?

CHAPTER 72: QUANTUM ENTANGLEMENT AND TELEPORTATION: NOSTRADAMUS'S VISIONS OF A CONNECTED UNIVERSE

While Nostradamus's prophecies often deal with earthly affairs, some of his quatrains hint at a future where humanity harnesses the enigmatic powers of quantum entanglement and teleportation. Despite living in the 16th century, Nostradamus's words resonate with cutting-edge scientific research in the 21st century, prompting us to ponder the potential implications of quantum technologies for communication, transportation, and our understanding of the universe.

The "Hidden Connection" and the "Instantaneous Passage"

In Century I, Quatrain 48, Nostradamus writes:

_The great plague in the maritime city.

Will not cease until there be avenged the death,
Of the just blood, condemned for a price without crime,
Of the great lady outraged by pretence._
While this quatrain often evokes images of disease and conflict, some interpretations suggest a connection to quantum entanglement. The "great lady outraged by pretence" could be seen as a metaphor for the fundamental interconnectedness of particles, even when separated by vast distances. This "hidden connection" could represent the quantum entanglement phenomenon, where the state of one particle instantaneously affects the state of another, regardless of the distance between them.

In Century IX, Quatrain 43, Nostradamus mentions a "king" who will "travel through the air and sea." This could be interpreted as a prediction of instantaneous travel, possibly through teleportation, a theoretical concept enabled by quantum entanglement.

Quantum Physics: Bridging the Gap between Nostradamus and Modern Science

In the realm of modern physics, quantum entanglement is a well-established phenomenon, with numerous experiments confirming its existence. Scientists are actively exploring its potential applications in fields such as quantum communication and quantum computing.

Teleportation, while still a theoretical concept, is also being actively researched. Scientists have successfully teleported photons and even atoms over short distances, but teleporting larger objects or humans remains a distant dream.

Nostradamus's prophecies, while not scientifically precise, resonate with these ongoing scientific endeavour s. His verses, with their references to "hidden connections" and "instantaneous passage," capture the enigmatic nature of quantum phenomena and their potential to revolutionize our understanding of the universe.

Potential Applications and Societal Implications

The development of quantum communication technologies

could revolutionize the way we transmit information, enabling secure and instantaneous communication across vast distances. This could have far-reaching implications for fields such as cryptography, finance, and national security.

Quantum teleportation, if realized, could transform transportation and logistics, enabling the instantaneous movement of people and goods across the globe. This could revolutionize global trade, tourism, and even warfare.

However, the development of quantum technologies also raises ethical concerns and potential risks. The ability to manipulate quantum states could lead to the creation of powerful weapons or the surveillance of individuals on an unprecedented scale. It is essential to carefully consider the potential consequences of these technologies and to develop ethical frameworks to guide their responsible use.

A Nostradamian Perspective on Quantum Advancements

Nostradamus's prophecies, while open to interpretation, offer a unique lens through which to view the potential impact of quantum technologies. They challenge us to envision a future where communication and transportation are revolutionized, where the boundaries of space and time are blurred, and where the very nature of reality is called into question.

As we delve deeper into the mysteries of the quantum realm, Nostradamus's verses remind us of the power of human curiosity and the potential for scientific discovery to transform our world. However, they also caution us to approach these advancements with humility and a keen awareness of their potential consequences.

Questions for Reflection:

1. How do Nostradamus's prophecies about quantum phenomena resonate with current scientific research and technological developments?

2. What are the potential benefits and risks of quantum communication and teleportation?

3. How can we ensure that the development of quantum technologies is guided by ethical principles and

serves the betterment of humanity?

CHAPTER 73: THE EVOLUTION OF HUMAN SENSES: NOSTRADAMUS'S VISIONS OF PERCEPTION BEYOND THE VEIL

In the enigmatic verses of Nostradamus, we encounter tantalizing hints of a future where human perception transcends the limitations of our five traditional senses. While his 16th-century perspective could not have envisioned the technological marvels of today, his cryptic prophecies resonate with contemporary explorations into sensory augmentation, the potential for new sensory experiences, and the evolving understanding of human consciousness.

The "Hidden Senses" and the "New Perception"

In Century I, Quatrain 50, Nostradamus writes:

"The lost thing is discovered, hidden for many centuries,

Pastor will be honoured as a demigod,

Before the Moon completes its full cycle,

By other winds he will be dishonoured."

While this quatrain has been interpreted in various ways, some scholars suggest that it could be a metaphor for the discovery of hidden or latent sensory capabilities within humans. The "lost thing" could represent these untapped senses, while the "pastor" could symbolize a scientist or researcher who unlocks their potential.

In Century II, Quatrain 27, Nostradamus speaks of a "divine word" that will give "all power" to the "body, soul, and spirit." This could be interpreted as a reference to the interconnectedness of our senses and the potential for enhanced perception through spiritual or technological means.

Sensory Augmentation: A 21st-Century Reality

In the realm of science and technology, researchers are exploring ways to augment our existing senses and even create new ones. Cochlear implants that restore hearing, retinal implants that provide artificial vision, and haptic feedback devices that enable tactile sensations in virtual reality are just a few examples of how technology is expanding our sensory horizons.

Nostradamus's prophecies, while not explicitly mentioning these specific technologies, could be seen as foreshadowing this trend towards sensory augmentation. The "new engine" mentioned in Century I, Quatrain 87, could represent a technological breakthrough that enables us to perceive the world in ways we never thought possible.

The Potential for New Sensory Experiences

As technology continues to advance, the possibilities for sensory augmentation seem limitless. Scientists are exploring the potential for sensory substitution, where one sense is used to compensate for the loss of another, as well as the creation of entirely new senses, such as the ability to perceive magnetic fields or infrared radiation.

Nostradamus's prophecies, with their cryptic references to "seeing the unseen" and "hearing the unheard," could be interpreted as hinting at these potential developments. The emergence of new sensory experiences could revolutionize our understanding of the world and ourselves, opening up new avenues for creativity, communication, and exploration.

The Ethical Implications of Sensory Augmentation

While the prospect of enhanced or new senses is undoubtedly exciting, it also raises important ethical considerations. How would our society change if we could perceive the world in entirely new ways? Would it lead to greater empathy and understanding, or would it create new forms of inequality and discrimination?

Nostradamus's prophecies, with their warnings of "great misfortunes" and "terrible events," serve as a reminder of the potential dangers of unchecked technological progress. As we explore the possibilities of sensory augmentation, it is crucial to consider the ethical implications and ensure that these technologies are used responsibly and for the benefit of all.

A Nostradamian Perspective on Sensory Evolution

Nostradamus's prophecies, while open to interpretation, offer a unique and thought-provoking perspective on the evolution of human senses. They challenge us to envision a future where our perception of the world is expanded beyond the limitations of our current senses, where technology enhances our understanding of reality, and where the boundaries between the physical and the digital are blurred.

As we navigate this uncharted territory, Nostradamus's verses remind us of the importance of embracing diversity, questioning our assumptions, and approaching technological advancements with caution and wisdom. By doing so, we can create a future where sensory enhancement serves to enrich our lives, deepen our understanding of the world, and foster a more inclusive and compassionate society.

CHAPTER 74: REDISCOVERING EARTH'S HIDDEN SECRETS: NOSTRADAMUS'S VISIONS OF UNEXPLORED REALMS

The Earth, our home planet, still holds countless mysteries in its depths and unexplored corners. While scientific exploration has shed light on many of these secrets, there are still vast realms that remain shrouded in darkness and intrigue. Nostradamus, with his enigmatic prophecies, offers a unique perspective on these hidden realms, suggesting the possibility of ground-breaking discoveries in deep-sea and subterranean environments that could reshape our understanding of Earth's ecosystems and our place within them.

The "Caverns of the Earth" and the "Abyss of the Sea"
Nostradamus, in Century VI, Quatrain 21, writes:

_The trembling of the earth at Mortara,
Cassiterides will be near the submerged,
Peace unassured, war will commence by sea and land,
Great will be the invasion from the East to the West._
While this quatrain primarily focuses on conflict and upheaval, the mention of "Cassiterides near the submerged" has sparked intrigue among interpreters. The Cassiterides, believed to be ancient islands off the coast of Europe, could be seen as a metaphor for submerged landmasses or hidden underwater realms. Some speculate that this could refer to the discovery of ancient civilizations or previously unknown ecosystems in the depths of the ocean.

In Century IV, Quatrain 67, Nostradamus speaks of "a great cave" that will be opened, revealing "treasures hidden for centuries." This could be interpreted as a prediction of the exploration of vast underground caverns and cave systems, potentially containing unique geological formations, fossils, or even evidence of past life forms.

Delving into the Depths: Unravelling Earth's Mysteries

In the 21st century, scientific exploration is pushing the boundaries of our understanding of Earth's hidden realms. Deep-sea submersibles are venturing into the ocean's abyssal plains, uncovering bizarre creatures and ecosystems that thrive in extreme conditions. Meanwhile, cave explorers are mapping vast underground networks, revealing hidden rivers, lakes, and even entire underground cities.

Nostradamus's prophecies, while not offering a detailed roadmap, resonate with these ongoing explorations. His verses, with their references to "submerged lands" and "hidden treasures," spark our imagination and encourage us to delve deeper into the mysteries of our planet.

The Impact on Our Understanding of Earth's Ecosystems

The discovery of new ecosystems and species in the deep ocean and subterranean environments could revolutionize our understanding of life on Earth. It could challenge our assumptions about the conditions necessary for life to thrive and shed light on the evolution of organisms in extreme environments.

For example, the discovery of extremophiles, organisms that thrive in harsh environments such as hydrothermal vents and acidic caves, has expanded our understanding of the diversity of life and its potential for adaptation. These discoveries could also have implications for astrobiology, the study of life beyond Earth, as they provide clues about the potential for life to exist in extreme environments on other planets.

The Nostradamian Perspective on Earth's Hidden Secrets

Nostradamus's prophecies, while open to interpretation, offer a unique perspective on the ongoing exploration of Earth's hidden realms. They encourage us to embrace curiosity, to seek out the unknown, and to challenge our preconceived notions about the limits of life.

As we venture into the depths of the ocean and the subterranean world, Nostradamus's verses remind us of the vastness and complexity of our planet. They also inspire us to approach these explorations with a sense of wonder and respect for the delicate ecosystems that we may encounter.

Questions for Reflection:

1.   How do Nostradamus's prophecies about hidden realms on Earth relate to current scientific explorations of the deep ocean and subterranean environments?

2.   What are the potential implications of discovering new ecosystems and species in these environments?

3.   How can we ensure that our exploration of Earth's hidden secrets is conducted in a responsible and sustainable manner?

CHAPTER 75:
THE FUTURE OF HUMAN CREATIVITY: NOSTRADAMUS'S VISION OF ART AND INNOVATION IN THE 21ST CENTURY

In the tapestry of Nostradamus's prophetic verses, we find intriguing threads that intertwine with the ever-evolving world of human creativity. While the 16th-century seer could not have envisioned the technological advancements and cultural shifts of our time, his enigmatic quatrains resonate with contemporary discussions about the role of artificial intelligence (AI) in artistic creation, the emergence of new forms of expression, and the enduring power of human imagination.

The "Hidden Muse" and the "New Renaissance"

Nostradamus, in Century I, Quatrain 63, writes of a "hidden art" that will be revealed, leading to a "renewal of the world." This quatrain, often interpreted in the context of scientific or technological breakthroughs, could also be seen as a metaphor for the unleashing of untapped creative potential within humanity. The "hidden art" could represent new forms of artistic expression, enabled by emerging technologies or inspired by a deeper understanding of the human mind and spirit.

In Century II, Quatrain 29, Nostradamus speaks of a "new law" that will "occupy the great world," bringing about a "golden age." This could be interpreted as a prediction of a cultural renaissance, where creativity flourishes and new artistic movements challenge established norms.

The Rise of AI in Artistic Creation

In the 21st century, we are witnessing the increasing use of AI in various creative fields, from music composition and visual arts to writing and poetry. AI algorithms can analyze vast amounts of data, identify patterns, and generate novel creative outputs that mimic and even surpass human creations in some instances.

Nostradamus, in Century III, Quatrain 97, speaks of a "new order of the centuries" that will bring about "great inventions." This could be interpreted as a foreshadowing of the rise of AI as a creative tool, enabling artists to explore new frontiers of expression and push the boundaries of human imagination.

However, the growing role of AI in creative processes also raises questions about the nature of authorship and the value of human creativity. Can a machine truly be creative? What is the role of human artists in a world where algorithms can generate art, music, and literature?

The Emergence of New Artistic Expressions

As technology continues to evolve, new forms of artistic expression are emerging that challenge traditional notions of art and creativity. Virtual reality (VR) art, interactive installations, and bio-art are just a few examples of how artists are leveraging technology to create immersive and thought-provoking experiences.

Nostradamus's prophecies, with their cryptic references to "strange enterprises" and "new forms," could be seen as hinting at these emerging trends. His verses encourage us to embrace innovation and explore new possibilities in artistic expression, while also reminding us of the enduring power of human creativity and the importance of preserving our cultural heritage.

A Nostradamian Perspective on the Future of Creativity

Nostradamus's prophecies, while open to interpretation, offer a unique lens through which to view the evolving landscape of human creativity. They challenge us to envision a future where art and technology intertwine, where new forms of expression emerge, and where the human imagination remains a boundless source of inspiration and innovation.

As we navigate the complexities of the 21st century, Nostradamus's verses remind us of the importance of nurturing creativity, embracing diversity, and fostering a culture that values artistic expression in all its forms. By doing so, we can ensure that the future of human creativity is not defined by machines but rather by the boundless potential of the human spirit.

Questions for Reflection:

1. How do Nostradamus's prophecies about art and creativity resonate with current trends in the arts and technology?

2. What are the potential benefits and risks of using AI in creative processes?

3. How can we support and nurture human creativity in a world where technology is increasingly intertwined with artistic expression?

As we contemplate these questions, we are reminded that creativity is not just a product of individual genius but also a reflection of our collective values, aspirations, and cultural identities. By embracing innovation, fostering diversity, and celebrating the power of human imagination, we can create a future where art flourishes and enriches our lives in countless ways.

CHAPTER 76: GLOBAL LANGUAGE AND CULTURAL PRESERVATION: NOSTRADAMUS'S VISION OF A WORLD IN FLUX

In the tapestry of Nostradamus's prophetic verses, we find threads that intertwine with the complex interplay of language, culture, and identity. While written in the 16th century, his quatrains resonate with contemporary concerns about the preservation of linguistic diversity, the impact of globalization on cultural traditions, and the delicate balance between interconnectedness and the preservation of unique identities.

The "Tower of Babel" and the "Universal Tongue"

Nostradamus, in Century X, Quatrain 74, writes of a time when "the great Empire of the Antichrist will begin" and "a single leader will rule the world." This quatrain, often interpreted as a prediction of global domination by a tyrannical figure, could also be seen as a metaphor for the homogenization of cultures and the erosion of linguistic diversity in the face of globalization.

The "Tower of Babel" is a biblical story that symbolizes the confusion of languages and the division of humanity. Nostradamus's reference to this story could be seen as a warning about the dangers of cultural assimilation and the loss of unique identities.

However, other quatrains hint at the possibility of a "universal tongue," a language that transcends cultural boundaries and fosters global understanding. In Century II, Quatrain 29, Nostradamus speaks of a "new law" that will "occupy the great world," bringing about "peace and harmony." This could be interpreted as a prediction of a future where communication barriers are overcome, and a shared language facilitates cooperation and understanding among diverse cultures.

The Preservation of Endangered Languages and Traditions

In the 21st century, the world is witnessing an unprecedented loss of linguistic and cultural diversity. According to UNESCO, a language dies every two weeks, taking with it a wealth of knowledge, traditions, and cultural expressions. This loss is driven by various factors, including globalization, urbanization, and the dominance of major languages like English, Spanish, and Mandarin.

Nostradamus's prophecies, while not explicitly mentioning endangered languages, could be seen as a call to action for their preservation. His verses remind us of the importance of cultural diversity and the richness of human expression that is embedded in different languages and traditions.

In recent years, there has been a growing movement to revitalize endangered languages and preserve cultural heritage. Organizations like UNESCO and the Endangered Language Alliance are working to document and revitalize threatened languages, while communities around the world are striving to maintain their unique traditions and customs in the face of globalization.

The Balance Between Globalization and Cultural Identity

The tension between globalization and cultural identity is a complex and ongoing challenge. While globalization has brought about increased interconnectedness, economic growth, and cultural exchange, it has also led to the homogenization of cultures and the erosion of traditional values.

Nostradamus's prophecies, with their warnings of "great changes" and "new orders," could be seen as reflecting this tension. His verses challenge us to find a balance between embracing the benefits of globalization and preserving the diversity of human cultures.

The Nostradamian Perspective on Global Language and Culture

Nostradamus's prophecies, while open to interpretation, offer a unique perspective on the evolving relationship between language, culture, and identity. They remind us of the importance of linguistic diversity, the need to preserve cultural heritage, and the challenge of finding a balance between globalization and local traditions.

As we navigate the complexities of the 21st century, Nostradamus's verses encourage us to embrace diversity, celebrate cultural differences, and promote cross-cultural understanding. By doing so, we can create a world where globalization enriches, rather than diminishes, the tapestry of human cultures.

Questions for Reflection:

1.	How do Nostradamus's prophecies about language and culture resonate with current debates about globalization and cultural preservation?

2.	What are the potential benefits and risks of a universal language?

3.	How can we promote linguistic and cultural diversity in an increasingly interconnected world?

CHAPTER 77: ADVANCEMENTS IN ROBOTICS AND AUTOMATION: NOSTRADAMUS'S VISION OF A MECHANIZED WORLD

Although Nostradamus lived centuries before the advent of robotics and automation, his cryptic verses offer a unique perspective on the growing role of machines in our lives. While the 16th-century seer could not have foreseen the intricacies of modern technology, his prophecies resonate with contemporary anxieties and aspirations regarding the integration of artificial intelligence and robotics into society.

The "Iron Men" and the "New Masters"

Nostradamus, in Century I, Quatrain 87, writes:

_The new engine will cause great riches to change masters,
Raised to heights, the bold one will be lowered by fortune._

This quatrain has been interpreted in various ways, but some scholars suggest it could allude to the rise of robots and automation, with the "new engine" representing these advanced technologies. The phrase "great riches to change masters" could be seen as a reference to the economic shifts caused by automation, while the "bold one lowered by fortune" might foreshadow potential risks associated with the widespread adoption of robots.

In Century II, Quatrain 41, Nostradamus describes a "new creature" that will emerge from the earth, causing "great terror and confusion." Some interpretations link this to the creation of human-like robots or artificial intelligence that could challenge our understanding of what it means to be human.

The Rise of Robots and Automation in 2024

As of 2024, robots and automation are increasingly integrated into various aspects of our lives. From manufacturing and logistics to healthcare and customer service, machines are taking on tasks that were once the exclusive domain of humans. This trend is driven by factors such as cost efficiency, productivity, and safety.

However, the rise of robots also raises concerns about job displacement, economic inequality, and the potential for machines to surpass human capabilities in various domains. The COVID-19 pandemic has further accelerated the adoption of automation in many industries, as businesses seek to reduce their reliance on human labour and adapt to new social distancing measures.

Nostradamus's prophecies, while not explicitly mentioning robots, could be seen as foreshadowing the potential consequences of this technological revolution. His verses, with their warnings of "great upheavals" and "changing times," resonate with the anxieties and uncertainties surrounding the growing role of machines in our society.

The Ethical Implications of Human-Robot Interactions

As robots become more sophisticated and integrated into our lives, the ethical implications of human-robot interactions become increasingly important. Should robots be granted rights or legal personhood? How do we ensure that AI-powered machines are used ethically and responsibly? What are the potential consequences of overreliance on automation for our social fabric and human connection?

Nostradamus's prophecies, with their cryptic references to "new creatures" and "changing laws," invite us to ponder these ethical questions. His verses, while not providing clear answers, challenge us to consider the potential impact of robotics and automation on our values, beliefs, and societal structures.

A Nostradamian Perspective on Robotics and Automation

Nostradamus's prophecies, while open to interpretation, offer a unique lens through which to view the ongoing integration of robots and automation into our lives. They remind us of the potential for both progress and peril, and encourage us to approach these technologies with caution, foresight, and a deep respect for human values.

As we navigate this uncharted territory, Nostradamus's verses challenge us to consider the following questions:

1. How can we ensure that the benefits of robotics and automation are shared equitably, and that technological advancements do not exacerbate existing inequalities?

2. What are the ethical boundaries of human-robot interactions, and how can we ensure that AI-powered machines are used responsibly and for the betterment of humanity?

3. How can we adapt our education systems and workforce development programs to prepare for a future where humans and machines work collaboratively?

By engaging in thoughtful dialogue, embracing a multidisciplinary approach, and prioritizing ethical considerations, we can navigate the challenges and opportunities of the robotic age, ensuring that technology serves to enhance human potential and create a more equitable and sustainable future for all.

CHAPTER 78: THE TRANSFORMATION OF HUMAN NUTRITION: NOSTRADAMUS'S VISION OF FOOD AND SUSTENANCE IN THE 21ST CENTURY

Nostradamus's prophecies, while often cantered on war, politics, and natural disasters, also offer intriguing glimpses into the future of food and nutrition. His cryptic verses, written in the 16th century, resonate with contemporary concerns about food security, the impact of technology on our diets, and the growing interest in personalized nutrition. This chapter delves into Nostradamus's enigmatic predictions, exploring their potential connections to innovations in food production, the rise of nutrigenomics, and the changing landscape of human nutrition.

The "Great Famine" and the "New Food"

In Century I, Quatrain 55, Nostradamus warns of a "great

famine" that will return to the world. This prediction, often interpreted as a harbinger of food shortages and agricultural crises, reflects the fragility of our food systems and the potential impact of climate change, conflict, and economic instability on global food security.

However, other quatrains offer a more optimistic outlook. In Century IV, Quatrain 67, Nostradamus speaks of "new foods" that will be "discovered in the earth." This could be interpreted as a prediction of innovative approaches to food production, such as vertical farming, lab-grown meat, and the development of alternative protein sources.

Personalized Nutrition and Nutrigenomics

In the 21st century, the field of nutrition is undergoing a revolution, driven by advances in genomics, data analytics, and personalized medicine. Scientists are uncovering the complex interactions between our genes, our diets, and our health, paving the way for personalized nutrition plans tailored to individual needs and preferences.

Nostradamus, in Century III, Quatrain 33, speaks of a "celestial fire" that will "descend from the heavens" and "cure all ills." While this quatrain is often interpreted in a spiritual context, it could also be seen as a metaphor for the transformative power of nutrigenomics, the study of how food affects our genes and health. By understanding our unique genetic makeup, we can tailor our diets to optimize health, prevent disease, and even slow down the aging process.

The Future of Food Production and Consumption

The way we produce and consume food is undergoing a radical transformation. The rise of factory farming, genetically modified organisms (GMOs), and ultra-processed foods has raised concerns about the environmental impact, health risks, and ethical implications of our current food system.

Nostradamus's prophecies, with their warnings of "famine" and "poisoned food," could be seen as a cautionary tale about the potential dangers of an industrialized and unsustainable food system. However, his verses also hint at the potential for positive change. In Century X, Quatrain 74, he speaks of a "new earth" where "abundance will reign." This could be interpreted as a prediction of a future where sustainable agriculture, regenerative farming practices, and a focus on locally sourced, whole foods become the norm.

The Nostradamian Perspective on Human Nutrition

Nostradamus's prophecies, while open to interpretation, offer a unique perspective on the evolving landscape of human nutrition. They challenge us to reconsider our relationship with food, to embrace sustainable practices, and to prioritize health and well-being over convenience and profit.

As we navigate the complexities of the 21st century, Nostradamus's verses remind us that food is not merely sustenance but also a source of medicine, pleasure, and cultural identity. By making informed choices about what we eat, where it comes from, and how it is produced, we can create a healthier, more sustainable, and more equitable food system for ourselves and future generations.

Questions for Reflection:

1. How do Nostradamus's prophecies about food and nutrition resonate with current trends and challenges in the field?

2. What are the potential benefits and risks of personalized nutrition and genetic engineering in food production?

3. How can we create a more sustainable and equitable food system that nourishes both people and the planet?

CHAPTER 79: NEW FRONTIERS IN MATHEMATICS: NOSTRADAMUS'S ENIGMATIC CLUES AND THE QUEST FOR MATHEMATICAL TRUTH

Nostradamus, a 16th-century scholar renowned for his cryptic prophecies, may seem an unlikely figure to offer insights into the world of mathematics. However, his verses, rich in symbolism and open to interpretation, have sparked intrigue among those who seek hidden meanings in his words. This chapter delves into Nostradamus's prophecies, exploring their potential connections to mathematical breakthroughs, the pursuit of solutions to long-standing problems, and the broader impact of advanced mathematics on various fields of study.

The "Hidden Calculations" and the "New Geometry"

In Century I, Quatrain 50, Nostradamus writes:

_"The lost thing is discovered, hidden for many centuries,
Pastor will be honoured as a demigod,
Before the Moon completes its full cycle,
By other winds he will be dishonoured."_
While this quatrain is often interpreted as a prediction of a political or religious figure, some scholars suggest that it could also allude to a ground-breaking mathematical discovery. The "lost thing" could represent a hidden mathematical principle or formula, while the "pastor" could symbolize a mathematician who unveils this knowledge.

In Century II, Quatrain 28, Nostradamus speaks of a "new geometry" that will "reveal the secrets of the universe." This could be interpreted as a prediction of advancements in geometric concepts and their applications in fields such as physics, cosmology, and architecture.

Mathematical Breakthroughs in the 21st Century

The 21st century has witnessed significant progress in various fields of mathematics, including number theory, topology, and chaos theory. The Riemann Hypothesis, a long-standing unsolved problem in mathematics, continues to captivate mathematicians and has potential implications for our understanding of prime numbers and their distribution.

Nostradamus's prophecies, while not providing explicit solutions to these mathematical puzzles, could be seen as foreshadowing the breakthroughs that await us. The "hidden calculations" and "new geometry" mentioned in his verses could represent the innovative approaches and tools that mathematicians are developing to tackle these complex problems.

The Interdisciplinary Impact of Mathematics

Mathematics, often referred to as the "language of the universe," plays a fundamental role in various fields of study. From physics and engineering to economics and biology, mathematical models and algorithms are used to describe, analyze, and predict phenomena.

Nostradamus's prophecies, with their cryptic references to

"numbers" and "calculations," could be seen as acknowledging the universal language of mathematics and its profound impact on our understanding of the world. The "new sage" mentioned in Century II, Quatrain 52, could represent a mathematician whose discoveries have far-reaching implications for multiple disciplines.

The Quest for Mathematical Truth: A Nostradamian Perspective

Nostradamus's prophecies, while open to interpretation, offer a unique perspective on the pursuit of mathematical truth. They challenge us to think beyond the boundaries of established knowledge and to embrace the power of intuition, creativity, and collaboration in solving complex problems.

As we navigate the complexities of the 21st century, Nostradamus's verses remind us that mathematics is not merely a tool for calculation but a language that can unlock the secrets of the universe. By embracing curiosity, fostering collaboration, and pushing the boundaries of our understanding, we can unlock new frontiers in mathematics and unravel the mysteries of the cosmos.

Questions for Reflection:

1. How do Nostradamus's prophecies about mathematics relate to current developments and challenges in the field?

2. What are some of the potential applications of advanced mathematics in other disciplines?

3. How can we encourage a greater appreciation for mathematics and its role in our understanding of the world?

CHAPTER 80: THE FUTURE OF HUMAN SPIRITUALITY: NOSTRADAMUS'S GLIMPSE INTO THE ETHEREAL REALM

Nostradamus, a man of profound faith and esoteric knowledge, often wove spiritual themes into his prophetic verses. While his quatrains remain shrouded in symbolism and open to interpretation, they offer a captivating glimpse into the potential evolution of human spirituality in the 21st century. This chapter explores Nostradamus's enigmatic prophecies, examining their relevance to contemporary spiritual movements, the intersection of science and spirituality, and the emergence of new beliefs and practices that may shape our understanding of the divine.

The "Celestial Fire" and the "New Religion"

In Century X, Quatrain 74, Nostradamus writes:

"The great man will be struck down in the day by a thunderbolt,

An evil deed foretold by the bearer of a petition,

According to the prediction another falls at night-time,

Conflict at Reims, London, and a pestilence in Tuscany."

While this quatrain is often interpreted as a prediction of political turmoil, some scholars suggest a deeper spiritual significance. The "thunderbolt" could symbolize a divine intervention or a sudden awakening of consciousness, leading to a transformation of religious beliefs and practices.

In Century III, Quatrain 97, Nostradamus speaks of a "new order of the centuries" that will usher in "great inventions" and "strange enterprises." This could be interpreted as a prediction of the emergence of new religious or spiritual movements that challenge traditional dogmas and offer alternative paths to enlightenment.

The Intersection of Science and Spirituality

In the 21st century, the boundaries between science and spirituality are becoming increasingly blurred. Quantum physics, with its concepts of entanglement and non-locality, has challenged our understanding of the nature of reality and opened up possibilities for a deeper connection between the material and spiritual realms.

Nostradamus, with his interest in astrology and alchemy, was a man ahead of his time, seeking to bridge the gap between science and spirituality. His prophecies, while often cloaked in religious imagery, can be interpreted as foreshadowing a future where scientific discoveries and spiritual insights converge, leading to a more holistic understanding of the universe and our place within it.

Emerging Spiritual Practices and Philosophies

In recent years, we have witnessed a resurgence of interest in ancient wisdom traditions, such as mindfulness, meditation, and yoga. These practices, rooted in Eastern philosophies, offer tools for self-awareness, stress reduction, and spiritual growth.

Nostradamus's prophecies, with their emphasis on inner peace, harmony, and the pursuit of knowledge, resonate with these emerging trends. In Century II, Quatrain 29, he speaks of a "new law" that will "occupy the great world," bringing about "peace and harmony." This could be interpreted as a prediction of a global shift towards greater spiritual awareness and the embrace of practices that promote inner peace and well-being.

The Nostradamian Perspective on Human Spirituality

Nostradamus's prophecies, while open to interpretation, offer a unique and thought-provoking perspective on the future of human spirituality. They challenge us to question established beliefs, explore new spiritual paths, and seek a deeper understanding of our place in the cosmos.

As we navigate the complexities of the 21st century, Nostradamus's verses remind us that spirituality is not confined to religious institutions or dogmatic beliefs. It is a dynamic and evolving aspect of human experience, shaped by our individual journeys, our cultural contexts, and our interactions with the world around us.

By embracing a spirit of openness, curiosity, and compassion, we can create a future where spirituality is a source of hope, healing, and interconnectedness, guiding us towards a more just, equitable, and sustainable world.

Questions for Reflection:

1. How do Nostradamus's prophecies about spirituality resonate with your own beliefs and experiences?

2. What role do you think science and technology play in our understanding of spirituality?

3. What new spiritual practices or philosophies do you see emerging in the 21st century?

CHAPTER 81: THE EVOLUTION OF HUMAN RIGHTS: NOSTRADAMUS'S VISION OF JUSTICE AND EQUALITY

Michel de Nostredame, the enigmatic Nostradamus, wrote his prophecies in an era marked by religious persecution, social inequality, and widespread human rights abuses. While his cryptic quatrains often focus on war, disaster, and political upheaval, some verses hint at a future where humanity strives for greater justice, equality, and the recognition of fundamental rights. As we delve into Nostradamus's prophecies, we explore their relevance to the evolving concept of human rights, the potential for technological advancements to empower individuals, and the ongoing struggle for a more just and equitable world.

The "Great Reset" and the "New Law"

In Century II, Quatrain 29, Nostradamus writes:

_The Eastern man will leave his seat,

To pass the Apennine mountains to see Gaul:

He will fly through the sky, the waters, and the snow,

And everyone will be struck with his rod._
While often interpreted as a prediction of a powerful leader from the East, this quatrain could also be seen as a metaphor for a global awakening to the importance of human rights. The "new law" could represent the emergence of international human rights norms and standards, while the "Eastern man" could symbolize the rising influence of non-Western cultures and their contributions to the global human rights discourse.

In Century III, Quatrain 97, Nostradamus speaks of a "new order of the centuries" that will bring about "great inventions" and "strange enterprises." This quatrain could be interpreted as a prediction of the rise of new technologies and social movements that challenge traditional power structures and empower individuals to claim their rights.

Expanding the Circle of Rights: Humans and Beyond

The concept of human rights has evolved significantly since Nostradamus's time. Today, we recognize a broad range of rights, including civil, political, economic, social, and cultural rights. The Universal Declaration of Human Rights, adopted by the United Nations in 1948, serves as a cornerstone of international human rights law, setting out fundamental rights and freedoms that all individuals are entitled to, regardless of their race, religion, gender, or nationality.

However, the question of who or what is entitled to rights is an ongoing debate. Some argue that rights should extend beyond humans to include animals, the environment, and even artificial intelligence. Nostradamus's prophecies, with their cryptic references to "new creatures" and "intelligent machines," could be seen as foreshadowing this expansion of the concept of rights to encompass non-human entities.

Technology as a Tool for Empowerment and Protection

Technological advancements have the potential to both empower and threaten human rights. On the one hand, technologies like the internet and social media have given individuals a platform to voice their concerns, organize protests, and demand accountability from governments and corporations. Biometric identification systems and blockchain technology could potentially enhance security and protect individual rights.

On the other hand, technology can also be used for surveillance, censorship, and social control. The rise of facial recognition software, data mining, and predictive policing algorithms raises concerns about privacy, freedom of expression, and due process. Nostradamus's prophecies, with their warnings of "great deceit" and "false prophets," could be seen as cautionary tales about the potential for technology to be misused to violate human rights.

The Nostradamian Perspective on Human Rights

Nostradamus's prophecies, while open to interpretation, offer a unique perspective on the evolving landscape of human rights. They challenge us to envision a future where rights are not only recognized but also protected and enforced, where technology is used to empower individuals rather than control them, and where the pursuit of justice and equality is a global endeavour .

As we navigate the complexities of the 21st century, Nostradamus's verses remind us that the struggle for human rights is ongoing and ever-evolving. By embracing diversity, promoting dialogue, and harnessing the power of technology for good, we can create a world where the rights of all individuals are respected, protected, and fulfilled.

CHAPTER 82: BREAKTHROUGHS IN ENERGY STORAGE: NOSTRADAMUS'S VISION OF A POWER-SHIFTING FUTURE

In the ever-evolving landscape of energy production and consumption, Nostradamus's enigmatic quatrains offer a glimpse into a future where energy storage and distribution undergo a dramatic transformation. While penned in the 16th century, his prophecies resonate with the challenges and opportunities presented by 21st-century advancements in battery technology, energy harvesting, and the integration of renewable energy sources into our power grids.

The "Hidden Fire" and the "New Sun"

In Century II, Quatrain 56, Nostradamus warns of "hidden fires" that will cause widespread destruction. While often interpreted as a prophecy of war or natural disaster, this quatrain could also be seen as a metaphor for the dangers of our reliance on fossil fuels and the potential for catastrophic consequences.

However, Nostradamus also hints at the emergence of a "new

sun" in Century X, Quatrain 74, which could be interpreted as a symbol of a new era of clean and sustainable energy. This prophecy resonates with the growing global movement towards renewable energy sources such as solar, wind, and hydropower.

The Rise of Battery Technology and Energy Harvesting

In 2024, the world is witnessing significant advancements in battery technology, with breakthroughs in energy density, charging speed, and cost-effectiveness. These innovations are critical for the widespread adoption of electric vehicles, renewable energy storage, and the development of microgrids that can provide power to remote communities.

Nostradamus's prophecies, while not explicitly mentioning batteries, could be seen as foreshadowing the importance of energy storage in the 21st century. The "hidden fire" could represent the potential for energy to be stored and harnessed in new ways, while the "new sun" could symbolize the transformative power of renewable energy coupled with efficient storage solutions.

Furthermore, the concept of energy harvesting, where energy is captured from ambient sources like sunlight, heat, or vibrations, is gaining traction as a sustainable way to power small electronic devices and sensors. Nostradamus, in Century IX, Quatrain 41, speaks of "iron birds" that will "draw power from the air." This could be interpreted as a prediction of energy harvesting technologies that harness the energy of the environment.

The Impact on Renewable Energy Adoption and Grid Stability

The integration of renewable energy sources into our power grids poses significant challenges due to their intermittent nature. Solar and wind power, for example, are dependent on weather conditions and may not always be available when needed.

Energy storage technologies play a crucial role in addressing this challenge, allowing excess energy to be stored during periods of high production and released when demand exceeds supply. This not only enhances the reliability of renewable energy but also contributes to grid stability and reduces the need for fossil fuel-based backup power.

Nostradamus's prophecies, with their warnings of "great changes" and "sudden reversals of fortune," could be seen as a cautionary tale about the potential disruptions that may accompany the transition to a renewable energy-based grid. However, his verses also hint at the potential for innovation and adaptation to overcome these challenges.

A Nostradamian Perspective on Energy Storage

Nostradamus's prophecies, while open to interpretation, offer a unique lens through which to view the evolving landscape of energy storage and its implications for the future. They challenge us to envision a world where energy is generated and stored in sustainable ways, where technological innovation drives progress, and where access to clean and reliable energy is a universal right.

As we navigate the complexities of the 21st century, Nostradamus's verses remind us of the importance of foresight, resilience, and a commitment to finding innovative solutions to the challenges we face. By investing in research and development, embracing new technologies, and fostering collaboration between governments, industry, and communities, we can create a more sustainable and equitable energy future for all.

Questions for Reflection:

1.	How do Nostradamus's prophecies about energy resonate with current developments in renewable energy and energy storage technologies?

2.	What are the potential benefits and challenges of integrating renewable energy sources into our power grids?

3.	How can we ensure that the transition to a sustainable energy future is equitable and accessible to all communities?

CHAPTER 83: THE FUTURE OF WASTE MANAGEMENT: NOSTRADAMUS'S WARNINGS AND THE QUEST FOR A ZERO-WASTE SOCIETY

While Nostradamus's prophecies are often associated with cataclysmic events, a closer examination reveals a subtle undercurrent of environmental concern. His cryptic verses, written in the 16th century, offer glimpses into a future grappling with the consequences of waste and pollution. In this chapter, we delve into Nostradamus's environmental prophecies, exploring their relevance to contemporary waste management practices, the potential for innovative solutions, and the path towards a more sustainable future.

The "Great Pollution" and the "Poisoned Earth"

In Century II, Quatrain 56, Nostradamus writes:

_In the year that Saturn and Mars are equally fiery,
The air very dry, a long comet,
From hidden fires a great place burns with heat,

Little rain, hot wind, wars, incursions._
While often interpreted as a prediction of war and natural disasters, this quatrain can also be seen as a warning about the devastating effects of pollution and environmental degradation. The "hidden fires" could symbolize industrial emissions, while the "hot wind" could represent the consequences of climate change, such as droughts and wildfires.

Nostradamus's prophecies, while not explicitly mentioning waste management, reflect a deep-seated concern for the health of the planet and the potential consequences of human activities. His verses serve as a reminder that our actions today will shape the world of tomorrow, and that we must prioritize sustainability and environmental stewardship to ensure a habitable future.

The Rise of Innovative Waste Management Solutions

In the 21st century, the world is witnessing a growing awareness of the environmental and health impacts of waste. Governments, businesses, and individuals are exploring innovative solutions to reduce, reuse, and recycle waste. From circular economy models that prioritize resource recovery to advanced recycling technologies that transform waste into valuable materials, the field of waste management is undergoing a paradigm shift.

Nostradamus's prophecies, with their cryptic references to "new inventions" and "strange enterprises," could be seen as foreshadowing the emergence of these innovative solutions. The "hidden gold" mentioned in Century I, Quatrain 49,could be interpreted as a metaphor for the potential value that can be extracted from waste through recycling and upcycling.

Towards a Zero-Waste Society

The concept of a zero-waste society, where waste is minimized and resources are reused or recycled, is gaining traction as a viable alternative to the current linear model of consumption and disposal. This approach not only reduces environmental impact but also creates economic opportunities and promotes social equity.

Nostradamus, in Century X, Quatrain 74, speaks of a "new earth" where "abundance will reign." This could be interpreted as a vision of a future where waste is seen as a resource, not a burden, and where sustainable practices are integrated into all aspects of our lives.

The Challenges and Opportunities of Waste Management

The transition towards a zero-waste society is not without its challenges. It requires a fundamental shift in our consumption habits, as well as significant investments in infrastructure and technology. However, the potential benefits are immense, ranging from reduced pollution and resource depletion to improved public health and a more sustainable economy.

Nostradamus's prophecies, with their warnings of environmental degradation and their hints of hope for a better future, serve as a reminder of the urgency and importance of addressing the waste crisis. They challenge us to think critically about our relationship with the environment and to embrace innovative solutions that prioritize sustainability and the well-being of future generations.

Questions for Reflection:

1. How do Nostradamus's prophecies about waste resonate with contemporary environmental challenges?

2. What are the most promising innovative waste management solutions being explored today?

3. What can individuals, businesses, and governments do to contribute to the creation of a zero-waste society?

CHAPTER 84: REDEFINING HUMAN INTELLIGENCE: NOSTRADAMUS'S VISION OF THE EVOLVING MIND

The enigmatic quatrains of Nostradamus, penned in the 16th century, offer glimpses into a future where human intelligence may undergo a profound transformation. While Nostradamus himself could not have envisioned the technological advancements and scientific discoveries of the 21st century, his cryptic verses resonate with contemporary discussions about cognitive enhancement, the impact of artificial intelligence (AI) on our understanding of intelligence, and the potential emergence of new forms of human cognition.

The "New Sage" and the "Hidden Knowledge"

In Century II, Quatrain 52, Nostradamus writes:

_The light of the moon at night over the high mountain,
The new sage with a lone brain sees it:
By his disciples invited to be immortal,
Eyes to the south. Hands in bosoms, bodies in the fire._

This quatrain, often interpreted as a prediction of lunar

exploration, could also be seen as a metaphor for the expansion of human knowledge and intelligence. The "new sage" could represent a visionary scientist or philosopher who unlocks the secrets of the human mind, while the "light of the moon" could symbolize the illumination of previously unknown aspects of cognition.

In Century III, Quatrain 97, Nostradamus speaks of a "new order of the centuries" that will bring about "great inventions." This could be interpreted as a prediction of breakthroughs in neuroscience, cognitive science, and artificial intelligence, which are already challenging our understanding of what it means to be intelligent.

AI and the Nature of Intelligence

In the 21st century, the development of AI has raised profound questions about the nature of intelligence. Can machines truly think and learn? What are the limits of artificial intelligence, and will it ever surpass human capabilities?

Nostradamus's prophecies, while not explicitly mentioning AI, could be seen as foreshadowing the emergence of intelligent machines that challenge our assumptions about human cognition. In Century I, Quatrain 87, he speaks of a "new engine" that will cause "great riches to change masters." This could be interpreted as a reference to AI, which has the potential to disrupt industries, automate jobs, and even reshape the global economic landscape.

The Evolution of Human Cognition: A Nostradamian Perspective

Nostradamus's prophecies, while open to interpretation, offer a unique lens through which to view the evolving nature of human intelligence. They challenge us to consider the potential impact of technology on our cognitive abilities, the ethical implications of cognitive enhancement, and the possibility of new forms of intelligence emerging through the integration of humans and machines.

As we navigate the 21st century, Nostradamus's verses remind us that the human mind is not a static entity but a dynamic and evolving system. Through education, experience, and technological augmentation, we have the potential to expand our cognitive horizons and unlock new realms of understanding.

The prophecies also caution us about the potential dangers of unchecked technological progress. As AI becomes more sophisticated, we must be mindful of the potential for it to be used for manipulation, control, or even the erosion of human autonomy.

Questions for Reflection

1. How do Nostradamus's prophecies about intelligence resonate with current debates about the nature of human cognition and the rise of artificial intelligence?

2. What are the potential benefits and risks of cognitive enhancement and the integration of humans with technology?

3. How can we ensure that the development of AI and other technologies serves to enhance human intelligence and promote a more just and equitable society?

As we contemplate these questions, we must remember that the future of human intelligence is not predetermined. It is up to us to shape it through our choices, our actions, and our commitment to lifelong learning and ethical decision-making. By embracing the possibilities of technological advancement while upholding the values of human dignity and autonomy, we can create a future where intelligence is not just a measure of cognitive ability but a reflection of our shared humanity and our capacity for compassion, creativity, and wisdom.

CHAPTER 85: THE TRANSFORMATION OF GLOBAL TRADE: NOSTRADAMUS'S VISION OF A SHIFTING ECONOMIC LANDSCAPE

As the world becomes increasingly interconnected, the dynamics of global trade are undergoing a profound transformation. Nostradamus, with his cryptic verses penned in the 16th century, may not have explicitly predicted the intricacies of modern commerce, but his prophecies offer intriguing insights into the potential shifts in economic systems, the role of emerging technologies like blockchain and cryptocurrencies, and the changing patterns of international trade.

The "Merchants of the East" and the "New Money"

In Century II, Quatrain 29, Nostradamus writes:

_"The Eastern man will leave his seat,

To pass the Apennine mountains to see Gaul:

He will fly through the sky, the waters and the snow,

And everyone will be struck with his rod._
While often interpreted as a prediction of a powerful leader from the East, this quatrain could also be seen as a metaphor for the rising economic power of Asian nations and their increasing influence on global trade. The "Eastern man" could represent emerging economies like China and India, while the "rod" could symbolize their economic clout and impact on global markets.

In Century I, Quatrain 87, Nostradamus speaks of a "new engine" that will cause "great riches to change masters." This enigmatic verse could be interpreted as a prediction of the emergence of new forms of currency and financial systems that disrupt traditional economic models. The rise of cryptocurrencies like Bitcoin and Ethereum, which operate outside of traditional banking systems, could be seen as a manifestation of this prophecy.

Blockchain and Cryptocurrencies: Disrupting Global Trade

In the 21st century, blockchain technology and cryptocurrencies are transforming the way we think about money, finance, and global trade. Blockchain, a decentralized and secure digital ledger, enables transparent and tamper-proof transactions, while cryptocurrencies offer an alternative to traditional fiat currencies.

Nostradamus's prophecies, while not explicitly mentioning blockchain or cryptocurrencies, resonate with the disruptive potential of these technologies. The "new engine" and the "new money" mentioned in his verses could be interpreted as foreshadowing the rise of decentralized financial systems and the potential for cryptocurrencies to reshape global trade.

Shifting Patterns of International Trade and Cooperation

The global trade landscape is undergoing a significant shift, with emerging economies like China, India, and Brazil playing an increasingly prominent role. The COVID-19 pandemic has further accelerated this trend, highlighting the vulnerabilities of global supply chains and the need for diversification and regionalization of trade.

Nostradamus's prophecies, with their warnings of "great upheavals" and "changing times," could be seen as anticipating these shifts in the global economic order. The rise of protectionism, trade wars, and the growing influence of non-Western powers all point towards a more multipolar world, where economic power is no longer concentrated in the hands of a few Western nations.

The Nostradamian Perspective on Global Trade

Nostradamus's prophecies, while open to interpretation, offer a unique lens through which to view the evolving landscape of global trade. They challenge us to reconsider our assumptions about economic systems, embrace new technologies, and adapt to the changing dynamics of international relations.

As we navigate the complexities of the 21st century, Nostradamus's verses remind us that the world is in constant flux. By staying informed about emerging trends, fostering collaboration, and promoting fair and sustainable trade practices, we can create a global economy that benefits all nations and individuals.

Questions for Reflection:

1.   How do Nostradamus's prophecies about global trade relate to current economic trends and geopolitical shifts?

2.   What are the potential benefits and risks of cryptocurrencies and blockchain technology for international trade?

3.   How can we promote a more equitable and sustainable global economic system in the face of increasing competition and complexity?

CHAPTER 86: ADVANCEMENTS IN WEATHER PREDICTION: NOSTRADAMUS'S GLIMPSE INTO THE EYE OF THE STORM

Nostradamus, the enigmatic 16th-century seer, is often associated with prophecies of apocalyptic events and natural disasters. While his quatrains are shrouded in symbolism and open to interpretation, some verses offer intriguing glimpses into the potential for advancements in weather prediction and their impact on our ability to prepare for and mitigate the effects of extreme weather events.

The "Fiery Heavens" and the "Changing Winds"

Nostradamus, in Century II, Quatrain 56, writes:

_"In the year that Saturn and Mars are equally fiery,

The air very dry, a long comet,

From hidden fires a great place burns with heat,

Little rain, hot wind, wars, incursions."_

This quatrain, often interpreted as a prediction of war

and natural disasters, could also be seen as a reference to extreme weather patterns and the challenges of predicting and adapting to them. The "fiery heavens" could symbolize the increasing intensity of heatwaves and wildfires, while the "changing winds" could allude to the unpredictability of storms and other meteorological events.

In Century I, Quatrain 69, Nostradamus writes:

"The dry earth will grow more parched, and there will be great floods when it is seen."

This quatrain, with its stark contrast between drought and deluge, could be seen as a foreshadowing of the erratic weather patterns associated with climate change, and the growing need for accurate and timely weather predictions to anticipate and mitigate their impacts.

The Rise of Meteorological Technology and Modeling

In the 21st century, weather prediction has undergone a remarkable transformation, thanks to advancements in satellite technology, supercomputing, and sophisticated modeling techniques. Meteorologists can now track weather patterns with unprecedented accuracy, providing early warnings of hurricanes, tornadoes, and other extreme events. Nostradamus's prophecies, while not explicitly mentioning these technologies, could be seen as hinting at the potential for human ingenuity to unravel the mysteries of the atmosphere and predict the weather with greater precision. In Century III, Quatrain 97, he speaks of a "new order of the centuries" that will bring about "great inventions." This could be interpreted as a reference to the development of new meteorological tools and models that enhance our ability to forecast and respond to weather events.

The Impact on Disaster Prevention and Resource Management

Accurate weather prediction is crucial for disaster prevention and mitigation. Early warnings of hurricanes, floods, and other extreme events can save lives and reduce economic losses. In addition, accurate forecasts of rainfall and temperature patterns can help farmers optimize crop yields and water resources, contributing to food security and sustainable development.

Nostradamus's prophecies, with their warnings of "great misfortunes" and "terrible events," serve as a reminder of the devastating impact of extreme weather events on human societies. However, they also hint at the potential for human ingenuity to harness the power of prediction and take proactive measures to mitigate the risks.

A Nostradamian Perspective on Weather Prediction

Nostradamus's prophecies, while open to interpretation, offer a unique perspective on the evolving science of weather prediction. They challenge us to consider the potential for both progress and peril in our quest to understand and control the forces of nature.

As we face the growing threat of climate change, Nostradamus's verses remind us of the importance of investing in scientific research, developing innovative technologies, and fostering international cooperation to enhance our ability to predict and respond to extreme weather events.

Questions for Reflection:

1. How do Nostradamus's prophecies about weather relate to current challenges in weather prediction and climate change?

2. What are the potential benefits and risks of geoengineering and other climate intervention technologies?

3. How can we use advancements in weather prediction to improve disaster preparedness and resource management?

CHAPTER 87:
THE FUTURE OF HUMAN MOBILITY: NOSTRADAMUS'S VISIONS OF A TRANSFORMED WORLD IN MOTION

Nostradamus, the enigmatic 16th-century seer, may not have envisioned bullet trains, hyperloops, or flying cars, but his cryptic verses contain intriguing allusions to a future where human mobility undergoes a profound transformation. While his prophecies are often shrouded in symbolism and open to interpretation, they resonate with contemporary developments in transportation technology and raise questions about the impact of these innovations on society and the environment.

The "Iron Bird" Takes Flight, Evolves, and Transforms

In Century IX, Quatrain 41, Nostradamus speaks of "iron birds" that will "traverse the sky." This verse, often interpreted as a prediction of the invention of airplanes, has been remarkably accurate. However, some scholars suggest that it could also foreshadow a broader revolution in transportation, where new modes of travel emerge, challenging traditional notions of mobility.

The 21st century has witnessed a rapid advancement in transportation technologies, with the rise of electric vehicles, autonomous drones, and the development of futuristic concepts like hyperloop and flying taxis. These innovations promise to revolutionize the way we travel, making transportation faster, safer, more efficient, and potentially more accessible.

Nostradamus's prophecy, while rooted in the past, could be seen as a glimpse into this transformative future. The "iron birds" of his vision may not only represent airplanes but also a broader array of aerial vehicles, from drones delivering packages to personal flying devices that could reshape urban commuting.

Beyond the Roads: Reimagining Personal and Mass Transit

In the 21st century, the concept of transportation is expanding beyond traditional cars and public transit systems. Electric scooters, shared bikes, and e-bikes are becoming increasingly popular in cities, offering a more flexible and sustainable alternative to car ownership.

Nostradamus, in Century VI, Quatrain 24, writes of a time when "the great cities will be overturned." This could be interpreted as a prediction of the decline of car-centric urban planning and the rise of more pedestrian- and cyclist-friendly cities. The development of micro mobility solutions like e-scooters and bike-sharing programs could be seen as a step towards this vision.

Meanwhile, advancements in mass transit systems, such as high-speed rail and hyperloop technology, promise to revolutionize long-distance travel. These technologies could not only reduce travel times but also decrease our reliance on fossil fuels and contribute to a more sustainable future.

Nostradamus's prophecies, while not explicitly mentioning these specific innovations, resonate with the idea of a transportation revolution that transcends the limitations of traditional modes of travel. The "new roads" and "strange vehicles" mentioned in his verses could be interpreted as foreshadowing the emergence of these futuristic transportation systems.

The Societal Impact of New Modes of Travel

The advent of new transportation technologies will undoubtedly have a profound impact on society. The rise of autonomous vehicles, for example, could lead to significant job displacement in the transportation sector, while also raising questions about liability and safety.

The widespread adoption of electric vehicles could reduce our reliance on fossil fuels and mitigate the effects of climate change, but it also requires a massive investment in infrastructure and a shift in consumer behavior.

Nostradamus's prophecies, with their warnings of "great upheavals" and "changing times," remind us that technological advancements are not without their challenges and potential drawbacks. However, they also offer a glimpse of a future where transportation is more efficient, sustainable, and accessible, transforming the way we live, work, and connect with each other.

The Nostradamian Perspective on Human Mobility

Nostradamus's prophecies, while open to interpretation, provide a unique lens through which to view the evolving landscape of transportation. They challenge us to think beyond the confines of our current systems and to envision a future where human mobility is redefined by innovation, sustainability, and a deep respect for the planet.

As we navigate this exciting yet uncertain terrain, Nostradamus's verses remind us that the future of transportation is in our hands. By embracing new technologies, investing in sustainable infrastructure, and prioritizing the needs of both people and the planet, we can create a world where transportation is a force for good, connecting us to new possibilities and empowering us to build a better future.

CHAPTER 88: REDEFINING THE CONCEPT OF NATIONALITY: NOSTRADAMUS'S VISION OF A BORDERLESS WORLD

Nostradamus, a man of the Renaissance era, lived in a world defined by rigid borders and distinct national identities. However, his enigmatic prophecies offer glimpses into a future where these traditional notions of nationality are challenged and transformed. In the 21st century, we are witnessing the rise of global citizenship, digital nomadism, and a growing awareness of the interconnectedness of humanity. Could Nostradamus's quatrains, with their cryptic references to shifting alliances and the fall of empires, be foreshadowing a redefinition of nationality in 2024 and beyond?

The "Great Wall" Crumbles and "New Alliances" Emerge

In Century I, Quatrain 50, Nostradamus writes:

"The lost thing is discovered, hidden for many centuries,

Pastor will be honoured as a demigod,

Before the Moon completes its full cycle,
By other winds he will be dishonoured."
This quatrain, often interpreted in the context of religious or political figures, could also be seen as a metaphor for the erosion of traditional boundaries and the emergence of new alliances. The "lost thing" could represent a sense of shared humanity that has been obscured by nationalistic ideologies, while the "pastor" could symbolize a leader who rises to prominence by promoting global cooperation and understanding.

In Century VIII, Quatrain 77, Nostradamus speaks of a "great war" that will "last for seven months." This prophecy has been linked to various historical conflicts, but it could also be interpreted as a warning of the dangers of nationalism and the need to transcend tribalistic identities to achieve lasting peace.

Global Citizenship and Digital Nomadism

In the 21st century, the rise of global citizenship and digital nomadism is challenging traditional notions of nationality. Global citizens identify with a global community and prioritize universal values over national interests. Digital nomads, untethered by geographic boundaries, embrace a lifestyle of mobility and cultural exchange.

Nostradamus's prophecies, with their emphasis on movement, change, and the interconnectedness of humanity, resonate with these emerging trends. In Century II, Quatrain 29, he speaks of a "new law" that will "occupy the great world," suggesting a shift towards a more globalized and interconnected society.

However, the rise of global citizenship and digital nomadism also raises questions about national identity, allegiance, and governance. How do we balance our loyalty to our home countries with our commitment to a global community? What are the implications of a world where individuals can easily relocate and work across borders?

New Forms of Governance and Political Structures

As traditional nation-states grapple with challenges like

climate change, global pandemics, and economic inequality, the need for new forms of governance and international cooperation becomes increasingly evident. Nostradamus's prophecies, with their cryptic references to "new kings" and "great empires," could be seen as foreshadowing the emergence of new political structures and alliances that transcend national borders.

The European Union, for example, is a supranational organization that has pooled the sovereignty of its member states in certain areas to achieve common goals. Could Nostradamus's prophecies be hinting at a future where similar organizations play a more prominent role in global governance?

The Nostradamian Perspective on Nationality

Nostradamus's prophecies, while open to interpretation, offer a unique perspective on the evolving concept of nationality. They challenge us to reconsider our attachments to nation-states, to embrace the interconnectedness of humanity, and to envision new forms of governance that can address the challenges of the 21st century.

As we navigate a world of increasing globalization and technological change, Nostradamus's verses remind us that identity is not static but rather a dynamic and evolving construct. By embracing our shared humanity, fostering cross-cultural understanding, and exploring new models of governance, we can create a more peaceful, just, and sustainable world for all.

Questions for Reflection:

1. How do Nostradamus's prophecies about nationality resonate with contemporary trends like global citizenship and digital nomadism?

2. What are the potential benefits and challenges of redefining our understanding of nationality?

3. How can we create a global community that respects both individual and collective identities?

CHAPTER 89:
THE EVOLUTION OF HUMAN SOCIALIZATION: NOSTRADAMUS'S GLIMPSE INTO THE SOCIAL WEB

Nostradamus, a keen observer of human nature, left behind a collection of cryptic verses that hint at the ever-evolving dynamics of human interaction. His 16th-century prophecies, while shrouded in symbolism and open to interpretation, resonate with contemporary discussions about the impact of technology on social structures, the changing nature of relationships, and the potential emergence of new forms of community and social organization.

The "Great Chatter" and the "Digital Tribes"

In Century I, Quatrain 67, Nostradamus speaks of a "great chatter" that will arise, followed by "great changes." This has been interpreted by some as a foreshadowing of the rise of the internet and social media, where communication and information exchange have reached unprecedented levels.

The digital age has indeed revolutionized human interaction, enabling us to connect with people from all corners of the globe and forming virtual communities based on shared interests and values. However, it has also raised concerns about the erosion of face-to-face interactions, the potential for online echo chambers, and the impact of social media on mental health.

Nostradamus's prophecies, while not explicitly mentioning social media, could be seen as anticipating the rise of "digital tribes" and the potential for both connection and isolation in the online world. His verses challenge us to reflect on the changing nature of community and the impact of technology on our social lives.

The "Fall of the Mighty" and the Rise of New Communities

In Century III, Quatrain 97, Nostradamus speaks of a "new order of the centuries" and the "fall of the mighty." This quatrain, often interpreted in the context of political upheaval, could also be seen as a prediction of the decline of traditional institutions and the rise of new forms of community and social organization.

In the 21st century, we are witnessing the growing popularity of co-living spaces, intentional communities, and online collectives that offer alternatives to traditional family structures and social networks. These new forms of community, often based on shared values, interests, or lifestyles, provide a sense of belonging and support in an increasingly fragmented and individualistic world.

Nostradamus's prophecies, with their cryptic references to "new alliances" and "strange enterprises," could be seen as hinting at the emergence of these innovative social structures. His verses encourage us to explore new ways of connecting with others and building communities that foster collaboration, creativity, and mutual support.

The Nostradamian Perspective on Human Socialization

Nostradamus's prophecies, while open to interpretation, offer a unique lens through which to view the evolving landscape of human interaction. They challenge us to reconsider our assumptions about social norms, to embrace the possibilities of technological connectivity, and to explore new ways of building community and fostering belonging.

As we navigate the complexities of the digital age, Nostradamus's verses remind us that human connection remains essential for our well-being and happiness. Whether we find community online or offline, in traditional or unconventional settings, the need for social interaction and mutual support is a fundamental aspect of human nature.

Questions for Reflection:

1.   How do Nostradamus's prophecies about social interaction resonate with your own experiences in the digital age?

2.   What are the potential benefits and drawbacks of online communities and virtual relationships?

3.   How can we leverage technology to foster deeper connections and build more resilient communities in the 21st century?

4.   What new forms of social organization do you see emerging in the coming years, and how might they reshape our understanding of community and belonging?

CHAPTER 90: BREAKTHROUGHS IN PAIN MANAGEMENT: NOSTRADAMUS'S VISIONS OF HEALING AND THE QUEST FOR A PAIN-FREE FUTURE

Throughout history, the alleviation of pain has been a fundamental human pursuit. Nostradamus, with his cryptic verses and enigmatic imagery, offers a unique perspective on this timeless endeavour . While his prophecies are shrouded in symbolism and open to interpretation, they resonate with contemporary research in pain management, hinting at potential breakthroughs in understanding pain mechanisms, developing innovative treatments, and addressing the ethical implications of altering human perception.

The "Great Suffering" and the "Balm of Gilead"

In Century II, Quatrain 6, Nostradamus writes:

_"Near the gates and within two cities

There will be scourges the like of which was never seen,

Famine within plague, people put out by steel,

Crying to the great immortal God for relief._
This quatrain, often interpreted as a prediction of widespread disease and suffering, could also be seen as a metaphor for the pervasive nature of pain and the human longing for relief. The "scourges" could represent chronic pain conditions, while the "crying to the great immortal God for relief" could symbolize the desperate search for effective treatments.

In contrast, Century IX, Quatrain 44, offers a glimmer of hope:
_"From the sky will come a great King of Terror,
To bring back to life the great King of Angoumois,
Before after Mars to reign by good luck."_
This quatrain, often interpreted in political or religious contexts, could also be seen as a prediction of a medical breakthrough that alleviates suffering. The "great King of Terror" could represent a disease or condition that causes widespread pain, while the "great King of Angoumois" could symbolize a new treatment or therapy that brings relief and restoration.

Novel Approaches to Understanding and Treating Pain

In the 21st century, scientists and researchers are exploring innovative approaches to pain management that go beyond traditional pharmaceuticals. These approaches include virtual reality therapy, mindfulness-based interventions, and neuromodulation techniques that target specific neural pathways involved in pain perception.

Nostradamus's prophecies, while not explicitly mentioning these specific technologies, could be seen as foreshadowing the development of new and unconventional treatments for pain. In Century III, Quatrain 97, he speaks of a "new order of the centuries" that will bring about "great inventions." This could be interpreted as a reference to the emergence of ground-breaking therapies that revolutionize the way we manage and understand pain.

Ethical Considerations in Pain Management

The ability to manipulate or eliminate pain raises complex ethical questions. While the relief of suffering is undoubtedly a noble goal, there are concerns about the potential for misuse of pain-altering technologies, such as the creation of "super soldiers" who can endure extreme pain or the suppression of emotional responses through chemical interventions.

Nostradamus's prophecies, with their warnings of "great misfortunes" and "terrible events," serve as a reminder that even well-intentioned interventions can have unintended consequences. As we develop new pain management techniques, it is crucial to consider the ethical implications and ensure that these technologies are used responsibly and for the benefit of all.

The Future of Pain Management: A Nostradamian Perspective Nostradamus's prophecies, while open to interpretation, offer a unique perspective on the ongoing quest to alleviate human suffering. They challenge us to think critically about the nature of pain, the role of technology in pain management, and the ethical considerations that arise as we seek to manipulate our perception of discomfort.

As we navigate the 21st century, Nostradamus's verses remind us that pain is a complex and multifaceted experience that encompasses both physical and psychological dimensions. By embracing a holistic approach to pain management, integrating conventional medicine with complementary therapies and addressing the underlying causes of pain, we can move towards a future where suffering is minimized and well-being is maximized.

Questions for Reflection:

1.   How do Nostradamus's prophecies about pain resonate with current developments in pain research and treatment?

2.   What are the potential benefits and risks of technological interventions in pain management?

3.   How can we ensure that the development and use of pain-altering technologies are guided by ethical principles and a commitment to human dignity?

CHAPTER 91: THE FUTURE OF INFORMATION VERIFICATION: NOSTRADAMUS'S WARNINGS OF DECEPTION AND THE QUEST FOR TRUTH

In an era of information overload and rampant disinformation, Nostradamus's prophetic verses resonate with a newfound urgency. While written in the 16th century, his quatrains offer cryptic glimpses into a future where truth and falsehood become increasingly intertwined, where manipulation and deceit threaten to undermine our trust in information sources. In this chapter, we delve into Nostradamus's prophecies, exploring their relevance to contemporary concerns about misinformation, the potential of technology to combat fake news, and the crucial role of critical thinking in navigating the digital age.

The "Great Deception" and the "False Prophets"

In Century III, Quatrain 81, Nostradamus warns:
The written word will be so obfuscated,
That no one will be able to understand it at all,
They will think they have seen the sun at night
When they will see the pig half man.

This quatrain, often interpreted as a prediction of widespread confusion and manipulation, could be seen as a foreshadowing of the current era of "fake news" and disinformation. The "obfuscated" written word could represent the deluge of misleading information online, while the "pig half man" could symbolize the blurring of boundaries between truth and falsehood.

In Century VIII, Quatrain 77, Nostradamus speaks of "false prophets" who will "deceive the masses." This could be interpreted as a warning about the dangers of propaganda, manipulation, and the intentional spread of misinformation for political or personal gain.

The Information War: A 21st-Century Reality

In the digital age, the battle for truth is being fought on a new frontier—the internet. Social media platforms, online forums, and even mainstream news outlets have become breeding grounds for misinformation, conspiracy theories, and propaganda. The rise of deepfakes, manipulated videos that can make anyone appear to say or do anything, further complicates the issue.

The consequences of misinformation can be devastating, eroding public trust, fuelling social unrest, and undermining democratic institutions. In the 2024 U.S. Presidential election, for example, the spread of false claims about voter fraud and election rigging has cast a shadow over the democratic process and sowed doubt in the minds of many citizens.

Technological Solutions for Fact-Checking and Authentication

In the face of this information war, technology is emerging as both a weapon and a shield. Fact-checking websites, such as Snopes and PolitiFact, use a combination of human expertise and algorithmic tools to verify the accuracy of claims and debunk false narratives. AI-powered tools are being developed to detect deepfakes and other forms of manipulated media.

Nostradamus, in Century IX, Quatrain 41, speaks of "iron birds" that will "traverse the sky." This could be interpreted as a reference to drones or other surveillance technologies that could be used to monitor and verify information in real time. While this raises concerns about privacy and surveillance, it also highlights the potential for technology to play a role in combating misinformation.

The Role of Critical Thinking and Media Literacy

While technology can be a valuable tool in the fight against fake news, the most powerful weapon we have is our own critical thinking skills. By questioning the sources of information, evaluating evidence, and considering multiple perspectives, we can become more discerning consumers of information and less susceptible to manipulation.

Nostradamus, in his writings, often emphasizes the importance of discernment and critical thinking. He warns against blind faith and encourages us to question authority and seek truth through our own intuition and reason.

The Future of Information Verification: A Nostradamian Perspective

Nostradamus's prophecies, while open to interpretation, offer a unique perspective on the challenges and opportunities facing us in the information age. They remind us of the importance of vigilance, critical thinking, and the pursuit of truth in a world where misinformation is rampant.

As we navigate the complexities of the digital landscape, Nostradamus's verses challenge us to be discerning consumers of information, to support independent journalism, and to advocate for policies that promote transparency and accountability. By doing so, we can create a future where truth prevails over falsehood, and where informed citizens can make decisions based on accurate and reliable information.

CHAPTER 92: ADVANCEMENTS IN MATERIALS SCIENCE: NOSTRADAMUS'S GLIMPSE INTO THE WORLD OF WONDER MATERIALS

Nostradamus, the enigmatic 16th-century seer, may not have explicitly predicted the advent of graphene, aerogel, or self-healing materials, but his cryptic verses contain intriguing allusions to a future where humanity harnesses the power of materials science to reshape the world around us. This chapter delves into Nostradamus's prophetic vision, exploring its potential connections to the development of new materials, the rise of smart materials and metamaterials, and the transformative impact these innovations could have on various aspects of our lives.

The "Philosopher's Stone" and the "Transformation of Matter"

In Century IV, Quatrain 33, Nostradamus writes:

_"The great man will come to the highest power,

He will raise the lowly and trouble the wicked,

He will transform all metals into gold,
And will cure all human diseases."_
This quatrain, often interpreted as a prediction of a powerful leader or a religious figure, could also be seen as a metaphor for the transformative power of materials science. The "great man" could represent a scientist or engineer who unlocks the secrets of matter, while the "transformation of metals into gold" could symbolize the creation of new materials with unprecedented properties.

In the 21st century, materials scientists are pushing the boundaries of what is possible, developing materials that are stronger, lighter, more durable, and more versatile than anything found in nature. From graphene, a one-atom-thick layer of carbon with extraordinary strength and conductivity, to aerogel, a lightweight material that is 99.8% air, these innovations have the potential to revolutionize industries ranging from electronics and energy to construction and medicine.

The Rise of Smart Materials and Metamaterials

Nostradamus's prophecies, while not explicitly mentioning smart materials or metamaterials, hint at a future where materials possess unprecedented capabilities. In Century IX, Quatrain 41, he speaks of "iron birds" that will "traverse the sky." This could be interpreted as a reference to the development of lightweight, high-strength materials that enable the construction of advanced aircraft and spacecraft.

Smart materials, which can change their properties in response to external stimuli, are already being used in various applications, from self-healing coatings for cars and airplanes to shape-memory alloys used in medical implants. Metamaterials, engineered structures with properties not found in nature, have the potential to revolutionize optics, acoustics, and even camouflage technology.

Applications in Construction, Manufacturing, and Daily Life

The advancements in materials science are already having a profound impact on our lives. New materials are being used to create stronger, lighter, and more energy-efficient buildings, improving sustainability and resilience in the face of climate change. In manufacturing, 3D printing and other additive manufacturing techniques are enabling the creation of complex and customized products with unprecedented speed and precision.

In our daily lives, we are already interacting with advanced materials without even realizing it. From the touchscreen on our smartphones to the lightweight frames of our bicycles, new materials are enhancing the performance, functionality, and aesthetics of the objects we use every day.

Ethical Considerations and the Path Forward

As we embrace the potential of materials science, it is crucial to consider the ethical implications of these advancements. The development of new materials, especially those with unique properties or potential for self-replication, raises questions about safety, environmental impact, and potential misuse.

Nostradamus's prophecies, with their warnings of "great misfortunes" and "terrible events," serve as a reminder of the importance of responsible innovation. As we explore the frontiers of materials science, we must proceed with caution, guided by ethical principles and a commitment to the well-being of both humanity and the planet.

A Nostradamian Vision for the Future of Materials

Nostradamus's prophecies, while open to interpretation, offer a unique perspective on the transformative power of materials science. They challenge us to envision a future where new materials shape our world, enhance our lives, and enable us to overcome the challenges of the 21st century.

By embracing innovation, prioritizing sustainability, and fostering ethical decision-making, we can harness the potential of materials science to create a more prosperous, equitable, and sustainable future for all.

CHAPTER 93: THE TRANSFORMATION OF LEGAL SYSTEMS: NOSTRADAMUS'S VISION OF JUSTICE IN THE 21ST CENTURY

In the labyrinthine verses of Nostradamus, we find enigmatic allusions to the transformation of legal systems, justice, and the very concept of law. While written in the 16th century, his prophecies resonate with contemporary debates about the impact of technology on legal processes, the evolving nature of crime and punishment, and the pursuit of a more equitable and just society. This chapter explores Nostradamus's prophetic vision, examining its potential connections to the rise of artificial intelligence in law, changing perceptions of crime and punishment, and the ongoing struggle for justice in an ever-changing world.

The "Law of the New World" and the "Fall of the Old Order"

In Century III, Quatrain 97, Nostradamus writes:

_The new order of the centuries will be renewed,
It will return to its high, heroic, and primeval state,
The great monarch will be restored by the favour of God,

The people will be happy and the world at peace._

This quatrain, often interpreted as a prediction of political change, could also be seen as a metaphor for the transformation of legal systems. The "new order of the centuries" could represent the emergence of new legal frameworks that challenge traditional notions of justice, while the "great monarch" could symbolize the rise of a new authority figure who champions fairness and equality.

In Century II, Quatrain 29, Nostradamus speaks of a "new law" that will "occupy the great world." This could be interpreted as a prediction of the rise of international law, human rights legislation, or other legal frameworks that transcend national borders and promote global justice.

Artificial Intelligence and the Law: A Nostradamian Vision?

The advent of artificial intelligence (AI) is transforming various industries, including the legal profession. AI-powered tools are being used to analyze vast amounts of legal data, predict case outcomes, and even draft legal documents. Some experts believe that AI could revolutionize the legal system, making it more efficient, accessible, and equitable.

Nostradamus's prophecies, while not explicitly mentioning AI, could be seen as foreshadowing the integration of technology into legal processes. In Century I, Quatrain 87, he speaks of a "new engine" that will cause "great riches to change masters." This could be interpreted as a reference to AI, which has the potential to disrupt the legal industry and shift power dynamics between lawyers, clients, and the courts.

Evolving Concepts of Crime, Punishment, and Rehabilitation

The traditional approach to crime and punishment, based on retribution and deterrence, is increasingly being challenged by alternative approaches that emphasize rehabilitation and restorative justice. These approaches recognize the complex social and economic factors that contribute to crime and seek to address the root causes of criminal behavior rather than simply punishing offenders.

Nostradamus's prophecies, with their emphasis on social

change and the "transformation of hearts," could be seen as anticipating this shift towards a more compassionate and holistic approach to justice. In Century IV, Quatrain 67, he writes of a time when "the hearts of men will change" and "mercy will prevail over vengeance." This could be interpreted as a prediction of a future where the legal system prioritizes rehabilitation and restorative justice over punitive measures.

The Future of Law and Justice: A Nostradamian Reflection

Nostradamus's prophecies, while open to interpretation, offer a unique lens through which to view the evolving landscape of law and justice. They challenge us to reconsider our assumptions about the role of law in society, the nature of crime and punishment, and the potential for technology to reshape the legal system.

As we navigate the complexities of the 21st century, Nostradamus's verses remind us that the law is not a static entity but a dynamic and evolving system that must adapt to the changing needs and values of society. By embracing innovation, promoting fairness and equality, and prioritizing human rights, we can create a legal system that truly serves the interests of justice and contributes to a more harmonious and equitable world.

Questions for Reflection:

1. How do Nostradamus's prophecies about law and justice resonate with current debates about the role of technology in the legal system?

2. What are the potential benefits and risks of using AI in legal processes?

3. How can we create a more just and equitable legal system that addresses the root causes of crime and promotes rehabilitation?

CHAPTER 94: REDEFINING HUMAN PRODUCTIVITY: NOSTRADAMUS'S VISION OF WORK, ACHIEVEMENT, AND PROGRESS

In an era of unprecedented technological advancement and societal change, the very concept of human productivity is being redefined. Nostradamus, the 16th-century seer whose cryptic quatrains have captivated and perplexed for centuries, offers intriguing insights into this evolving landscape. While his prophecies are often veiled in symbolism and open to interpretation, they resonate with contemporary discussions about the impact of automation on the workforce, the changing nature of work, and the need for new metrics to measure societal progress and success.

The "Iron Hand" and the "New Work"

In Century I, Quatrain 87, Nostradamus writes:

_"The new engine will cause great riches to change masters,
Raised to heights, the bold one will be lowered by fortune._

This quatrain, often interpreted in the context of political or economic upheaval, could also be seen as a metaphor for the transformative power of automation and technology. The "new engine" could represent AI and robotics, while the "great riches" could symbolize the wealth and power associated with productivity and labour.

The rise of automation has sparked fears of mass unemployment and economic disruption. However, it has also opened up new possibilities for human endeavour , freeing us from mundane tasks and allowing us to focus on more creative and fulfilling pursuits. Nostradamus's prophecy, while ambiguous, could be seen as foretelling this shift towards a new era of work, where human ingenuity and collaboration are valued above repetitive and manual labour.

The Balance between Automation and Human Contribution

In Century III, Quatrain 97, Nostradamus speaks of a "new order of the centuries" that will bring about "great inventions." This could be interpreted as a prediction of a future where automation and AI are seamlessly integrated into our lives, enhancing our productivity and improving our quality of life.

However, the quatrain also warns that "the old ways will be forgotten," suggesting that the transition to a more automated society will not be without its challenges. As machines take on more tasks, we must grapple with questions about the value of human labour, the importance of creativity and critical thinking, and the need to ensure that the benefits of automation are shared equitably.

The pursuit of a more harmonious balance between automation and human contribution is a central theme in contemporary discussions about the future of work. Some advocate for a universal basic income to provide economic security in a world where jobs are increasingly automated, while others emphasize the importance of education and reskilling to prepare workers for the jobs of the future.

New Metrics for Measuring Progress and Success

The traditional metrics of economic growth, such as GDP,

are increasingly being questioned as inadequate measures of societal well-being. In a world where automation and AI are reshaping the nature of work and productivity, we need new metrics that account for factors such as quality of life, environmental sustainability, and social equity.

Nostradamus, in Century II, Quatrain 29, speaks of a "new law" that will "occupy the great world," bringing about "peace and harmony." This could be interpreted as a prediction of a shift towards a more holistic and compassionate approach to measuring societal progress, one that values human flourishing and environmental sustainability over material wealth and economic growth.

The Nostradamian Perspective on Human Productivity

Nostradamus's prophecies, while open to interpretation, offer a unique lens through which to view the evolving nature of work and productivity. They challenge us to reconsider our assumptions about the value of labour, the role of technology in our lives, and the metrics we use to measure success.

As we navigate the complexities of the 21st century, Nostradamus's verses remind us that human potential is not limited to repetitive tasks and that true fulfilment lies in the pursuit of creativity, collaboration, and purpose. By embracing technological advancements while prioritizing human well-being and environmental sustainability, we can create a future where work is not just a means to an end but a source of meaning, purpose, and shared prosperity.

CHAPTER 95:
THE FUTURE OF GENETIC DIVERSITY: NOSTRADAMUS'S WARNINGS AND THE QUEST FOR PRESERVATION

Amidst Nostradamus's cryptic prophecies, a recurring theme emerges: a concern for the delicate balance of nature and the potential consequences of human intervention in the genetic makeup of living beings. While the 16th-century seer could not have foreseen the complexities of modern biotechnology, his enigmatic verses resonate with contemporary debates about genetic diversity, the ethical implications of genetic manipulation, and the ongoing efforts to preserve and restore biodiversity.

The "Unnatural Offspring" and the "Changing Forms of Life"

In Century II, Quatrain 41, Nostradamus warns of a "new creature" that will emerge, causing "great terror and confusion." This cryptic phrase has been interpreted by some as a foreshadowing of the rise of genetically modified organisms (GMOs) and other forms of synthetic life.

In Century VIII, Quatrain 55, he speaks of "unnatural offspring" that will "rise from the depths." This could be seen as a reference to the creation of new species through genetic engineering or the potential for unintended consequences arising from human manipulation of the genetic code.

While Nostradamus's prophecies lack the scientific precision of modern genetics, they nonetheless capture the essence of a growing concern about the impact of human actions on the diversity of life on Earth.

The Importance of Genetic Diversity in 2024

In 2024, the world is grappling with an unprecedented loss of biodiversity, driven by factors such as habitat destruction, climate change, and pollution. The loss of genetic diversity within species further exacerbates this crisis, making populations more vulnerable to disease, environmental change, and extinction.

The preservation of genetic diversity is essential for the health of ecosystems and the long-term survival of species. It provides the raw material for adaptation and evolution, allowing organisms to respond to changing environmental conditions and maintain their resilience.

Nostradamus's prophecies, with their warnings of "great plagues" and "unnatural creations," serve as a reminder of the potential consequences of tampering with the genetic makeup of living beings. They also highlight the importance of preserving genetic diversity to ensure the health and stability of ecosystems.

Efforts to Preserve and Restore Genetic Variety

In the 21st century, scientists and conservationists are working tirelessly to preserve and restore genetic diversity in both wild and domesticated populations. This involves efforts to protect endangered species, establish gene banks, and promote sustainable agricultural practices.

One promising approach is the use of genetic rescue techniques, where individuals from genetically diverse populations are introduced into declining populations to boost their genetic health and resilience. Another approach is de-extinction, the controversial practice of using genetic engineering to bring back extinct species, such as the woolly mammoth or the passenger pigeon.

Ethical Debates Surrounding Genetic Manipulation

The ability to manipulate the genetic code raises profound ethical questions about the boundaries of human intervention in the natural world. Should we create new species through genetic engineering? Should we attempt to revive extinct species? What are the potential consequences of altering the genetic makeup of organisms for future generations?

Nostradamus's prophecies, with their cryptic warnings and enigmatic imagery, do not offer easy answers to these complex questions. However, they do challenge us to think critically about the potential consequences of our actions and to approach the field of genetic engineering with caution and humility.

A Nostradamian Perspective on Genetic Diversity

Nostradamus's prophecies, while open to interpretation, offer a unique perspective on the importance of genetic diversity and the potential risks of human intervention in the natural world. They remind us of the delicate balance of ecosystems and the need for responsible stewardship of our planet's biodiversity.

As we navigate the 21st century, Nostradamus's verses encourage us to embrace a holistic and ethical approach to genetic research and conservation. By protecting endangered species, preserving genetic diversity, and carefully considering the implications of genetic manipulation, we can ensure a future where the wonders of the natural world continue to inspire and sustain us.

Questions for Reflection:

1. How do Nostradamus's prophecies about genetic diversity relate to current concerns about biodiversity loss and the ethical implications of genetic engineering?

2.	What are the potential benefits and risks of de-extinction and the creation of synthetic species?

3.	How can we balance the pursuit of scientific progress with the need to protect and preserve the natural world?

CHAPTER 96: BREAKTHROUGHS IN QUANTUM BIOLOGY: NOSTRADAMUS'S VISION OF LIFE'S HIDDEN MECHANISMS

The enigmatic prophecies of Nostradamus, steeped in the language of astrology and alchemy, may seem incongruous with the cutting-edge world of quantum biology. Yet, a closer examination of his cryptic verses reveals tantalizing hints that resonate with this emerging field. This chapter explores Nostradamus's prophetic vision, examining its potential connections to breakthroughs in our understanding of quantum effects in biological processes, the implications for medicine and biotechnology, and the broader philosophical questions raised by this interdisciplinary field.

The "Hidden Essence" and the "Invisible Hand"

In Century II, Quatrain 27, Nostradamus writes:

_The divine word will give to the substance,

Including heaven, earth, gold, hidden in the breast:

Body, soul, spirit having all power,
As much under its feet as the Heavenly Host above._
This quatrain, often interpreted as a spiritual or religious prophecy, can also be seen as a metaphor for the hidden forces that govern life. The "divine word" could represent the underlying laws of nature, while the "hidden" aspect could allude to the quantum realm, where particles behave in ways that defy classical physics.

In Century IV, Quatrain 67, Nostradamus speaks of "copies of gold and silver inflated." This could be interpreted as a reference to the complex molecular structures within living organisms, which are often made up of repeating patterns and intricate designs. These structures, like the "copies of gold and silver," could be governed by quantum principles that are only now beginning to be understood.

Quantum Biology: A New Frontier in Life Sciences

Quantum biology is an emerging field that seeks to understand how quantum mechanics, the branch of physics that deals with the behavior of matter and energy at the atomic and subatomic level, plays a role in biological processes. While classical physics explains much of the macroscopic world, quantum effects like superposition, entanglement, and tunnelling may be crucial for understanding the molecular mechanisms of life.

In recent years, scientists have discovered evidence of quantum effects in photosynthesis, bird navigation, and even the sense of smell. These findings suggest that quantum biology could revolutionize our understanding of life and lead to new breakthroughs in medicine, biotechnology, and other fields.

Potential Applications in Medicine and Biotechnology

Quantum biology has the potential to transform the way we diagnose and treat diseases. For example, researchers are exploring the use of quantum dots, tiny particles that exhibit quantum properties, for targeted drug delivery and medical imaging. Quantum sensors could also be used to detect diseases at an early stage, enabling more effective treatment.

In biotechnology, quantum biology could lead to the development of new biomaterials, biofuels, and synthetic organisms with enhanced properties. For example, researchers are investigating the use of quantum entanglement to create more efficient solar cells and to engineer microbes that can produce biofuels.

Ethical Considerations and Philosophical Implications

The emergence of quantum biology raises profound ethical and philosophical questions. If quantum effects play a crucial role in life, what does this mean for our understanding of consciousness, free will, and the nature of reality itself? Could quantum biology lead to new forms of human enhancement or even the creation of artificial life?

Nostradamus's prophecies, with their cryptic warnings and enigmatic visions, invite us to contemplate these complex questions. His verses, while not providing definitive answers, encourage us to approach the field of quantum biology with both curiosity and caution, recognizing its potential to both illuminate and transform our understanding of life.

A Nostradamian Vision for the Future of Quantum Biology

Nostradamus's prophecies, while open to interpretation, offer a unique perspective on the emerging field of quantum biology. They challenge us to envision a future where the boundaries between the living and the non-living, the biological and the technological, become increasingly blurred. As we delve deeper into the mysteries of life, Nostradamus's verses remind us of the interconnectedness of all things and the potential for new discoveries to reshape our understanding of the world around us. By embracing the interdisciplinary nature of quantum biology and exploring its ethical implications, we can pave the way for a future where science and technology are used to enhance human well-being and foster a deeper appreciation for the complexity and wonder of life itself.

CHAPTER 97: THE EVOLUTION OF HUMAN MORALITY: NOSTRADAMUS'S GLIMPSE INTO THE ETHICAL COMPASS OF THE FUTURE

Nostradamus, the 16th-century seer renowned for his cryptic prophecies, may seem an unlikely source for insights into the future of human morality. Yet, his enigmatic verses, often cloaked in symbolism and open to interpretation, offer a unique lens through which to examine the ever-evolving nature of ethical norms and values. This chapter delves into Nostradamus's prophetic vision, exploring its potential connections to contemporary debates about the impact of technology on moral reasoning, the emergence of new ethical frameworks, and the ongoing quest for a just and compassionate society.

The "Great Reset" and the "New Law"

In Century III, Quatrain 97, Nostradamus writes:

_The new order of the centuries will be renewed,

It will return to its high, heroic, and primeval state,
The great monarch will be restored by the favour of God,
The people will be happy and the world at peace._
This quatrain, often interpreted as a prediction of political change, could also be seen as a metaphor for a moral and ethical transformation. The "new order" could represent a shift towards a more just and equitable society, while the "great monarch" could symbolize a leader who champions ethical values and inspires moral renewal.

In Century II, Quatrain 29, Nostradamus speaks of a "new law" that will "occupy the great world." This could be interpreted as a prediction of the emergence of new ethical frameworks that address the challenges of the 21st century, such as climate change, inequality, and technological disruption.

The Impact of Technology on Moral Reasoning

Technology has transformed the way we interact with each other and the world around us, raising new ethical dilemmas and challenging traditional moral norms. The rise of artificial intelligence, genetic engineering, and social media has created a complex landscape where the boundaries between right and wrong are increasingly blurred.

Nostradamus, in Century I, Quatrain 87, speaks of a "new engine" that will cause "great riches to change masters." This could be interpreted as a warning about the potential for technology to be used for both good and evil, to empower and exploit, to connect and divide.

The development of AI, for example, raises questions about the ethical implications of creating machines that can make moral decisions. Should we trust algorithms to determine who gets a loan, who is eligible for parole, or even who lives or dies in a self-driving car accident? These are complex questions with no easy answers, but they underscore the importance of ethical reflection in the age of technology.

Emerging Ethical Frameworks for a Globalized World

As the world becomes more interconnected, the need for a global ethical framework becomes increasingly apparent. We must find ways to address challenges that transcend national borders, such as climate change, pandemics, and human rights abuses.

Nostradamus's prophecies, with their emphasis on universal values and the interconnectedness of humanity, resonate with this call for global ethical awareness. In Century VI, Quatrain 21, he speaks of a "great peace" that will be achieved through the "union of nations." This could be interpreted as a vision of a future where global cooperation and shared ethical principles guide our actions towards a more just and sustainable world.

The Nostradamian Perspective on Human Morality

Nostradamus's prophecies, while open to interpretation, offer a unique lens through which to view the evolving landscape of human morality. They challenge us to question our assumptions about right and wrong, to grapple with the ethical dilemmas posed by technological advancements, and to strive for a future where compassion, justice, and human dignity are paramount.

As we navigate the complexities of the 21st century, Nostradamus's verses remind us that morality is not a static concept but a dynamic and evolving force. By embracing ethical reflection, engaging in open dialogue, and fostering a sense of shared responsibility, we can create a world where moral values guide our actions and shape a more equitable and harmonious future for all.

CHAPTER 98: REDEFINING THE HUMAN-ANIMAL RELATIONSHIP: NOSTRADAMUS'S VISION OF INTERSPECIES HARMONY

Nostradamus, the 16th-century seer renowned for his cryptic prophecies, may seem an unlikely source for insights into the future of human-animal relationships. Yet, his enigmatic verses, often steeped in symbolism and allegory, offer a unique perspective on the evolving connection between humans and the animal kingdom. As we delve into Nostradamus's prophecies, we explore their potential relevance to contemporary discussions about animal cognition, animal rights, and the emergence of new forms of interspecies cooperation and understanding.

The "Beast of the Earth" and the "Wise Animals"

In Century VIII, Quatrain 55, Nostradamus writes:

_The trembling earth at Mortara,
Cassiterides will be near the submerged,
Peace unassured, war will commence by sea and land,
Great will be the invasion from the East to the West._
While this quatrain primarily focuses on conflict and upheaval, some interpret the mention of "beasts" as a reference to the animal kingdom. The "trembling earth" and the potential submersion of land could be seen as a warning of environmental destruction and the resulting impact on animal habitats. Others interpret this quatrain as a foreshadowing of a closer relationship between humans and animals, where animals play a more significant role in human affairs.

In Century II, Quatrain 27, Nostradamus speaks of a "divine word" that will give "all power" to the "body, soul, and spirit." This quatrain could be interpreted as a prediction of a new era of understanding and empathy between humans and animals, where we recognize their intelligence, emotions, and intrinsic value.

The Rise of Animal Cognition Research

In the 21st century, scientific research has revealed the remarkable intelligence and cognitive abilities of animals. Studies have shown that animals can use tools, solve complex problems, communicate with each other, and even exhibit emotions like empathy and grief.

Nostradamus's prophecies, while not explicitly mentioning animal cognition, resonate with these discoveries. His verses, with their references to "wise animals" and "hidden knowledge," could be seen as anticipating a future where we gain a deeper understanding of the animal mind and its potential.

Changing Attitudes Towards Animal Rights and Welfare

As our understanding of animal cognition grows, so too does the movement for animal rights and welfare. The 21st century has witnessed a growing awareness of the ethical implications of factory farming, animal experimentation, and the use of animals for entertainment.

Nostradamus's prophecies, with their warnings of "great misfortunes" and "terrible events," could be seen as a cautionary tale about the consequences of exploiting and mistreating animals. They also hint at the potential for a more harmonious and respectful relationship between humans and the animal kingdom.

The Future of Human-Animal Relationships: A Nostradamian Perspective

Nostradamus's prophecies, while open to interpretation, offer a unique perspective on the evolving relationship between humans and animals. They challenge us to reconsider our assumptions about animal intelligence, to explore new ways of communicating and interacting with other species, and to advocate for more ethical and sustainable treatment of animals.

As we navigate the 21st century, Nostradamus's verses remind us of the interconnectedness of all living beings and the importance of fostering a more harmonious relationship with the natural world. By embracing empathy, compassion, and respect for all forms of life, we can create a future where humans and animals thrive together in a balanced and sustainable ecosystem.

Questions for Reflection:

1.	How do Nostradamus's prophecies about animals resonate with current scientific research and ethical debates regarding animal rights?

2.	What are the potential implications of advancements in animal cognition research for our understanding of animal intelligence and consciousness?

3.	How can we promote a more compassionate and respectful relationship with animals in our daily lives?

CHAPTER 99: THE FUTURE OF HUMAN EXPLORATION: NOSTRADAMUS'S VISION OF A WORLD UNVEILED

In the cryptic verses of Nostradamus, a restless spirit of exploration and discovery emerges. While the 16th-century seer could not have fathomed the technological advancements that have propelled humanity to the depths of the ocean and the vast expanse of space, his enigmatic quatrains resonate with the enduring human drive to explore the unknown and push the boundaries of our understanding. This chapter delves into Nostradamus's prophetic vision, examining its potential connections to the future of human exploration on Earth, in the oceans, and beyond our planet.

The "New World" and the "Hidden Lands"

Nostradamus, in Century II, Quatrain 29, writes of a "new law" that will "occupy the great world," bringing about "peace and harmony." This quatrain, often interpreted in the context of political and social change, could also be seen as a metaphor for the discovery of new frontiers and the expansion of human knowledge. The "new law" could represent the scientific and technological breakthroughs that enable us to explore previously inaccessible realms, while the "great world" could symbolize the vastness of the universe and the endless possibilities for discovery.

In Century X, Quatrain 72, Nostradamus speaks of a "new king" who will "rise from the East" and "reveal hidden secrets." This could be interpreted as a prediction of a visionary leader who will inspire and guide humanity's exploration of new frontiers. The "hidden secrets" could represent the scientific, cultural, and spiritual treasures that await us in unexplored territories.

Terrestrial Exploration: The "Great Discoveries"

In the 21st century, the spirit of exploration is alive and well, with scientists and adventurers venturing into the most remote and inhospitable corners of our planet. From the depths of the Amazon rainforest to the icy plains of Antarctica, explorers are uncovering new species, geological formations, and archaeological sites that enrich our understanding of Earth's history and biodiversity.

Nostradamus's prophecies, with their cryptic references to "strange creatures" and "hidden lands," could be seen as foreshadowing these discoveries. His verses, while often veiled in symbolism, encourage us to embrace curiosity and wonder as we explore the last remaining frontiers on our planet.

Oceanic Exploration: The "Submerged Worlds"

The ocean, which covers over 70% of Earth's surface, remains a vast and largely unexplored frontier. In recent years, advances in underwater technology have enabled scientists to delve deeper into the ocean's depths, revealing astonishing ecosystems, hydrothermal vents teeming with life, and even the remains of ancient shipwrecks.

Nostradamus, in Century VI, Quatrain 21, speaks of "Cassiterides near the submerged," which some interpret as a reference to submerged landmasses or hidden underwater realms. Could this be a prediction of the discovery of

underwater cities, ancient artifacts, or even new forms of life?
Space Exploration: The "Celestial Chariots"
The 21st century is also witnessing a renewed interest in space exploration, with both government agencies and private companies investing heavily in missions to the Moon, Mars, and beyond. The dream of establishing a permanent human presence on other planets is no longer science fiction but a tangible possibility.

Nostradamus, in Century IX, Quatrain 41, speaks of "iron birds" that will "traverse the sky." This could be seen as a prediction of spacecraft and rockets, which are now essential tools for exploring the cosmos. His verses, with their references to "celestial chariots" and "starry messengers," could also be interpreted as foreshadowing the possibility of encountering extra-terrestrial life.

The Nostradamian Perspective on Human Exploration
Nostradamus's prophecies, while open to interpretation, offer a unique perspective on the future of human exploration. They challenge us to embrace the unknown, to seek out new knowledge and experiences, and to push the boundaries of what is possible.

As we venture into new frontiers, Nostradamus's verses remind us of the importance of humility, respect for the natural world, and a willingness to learn from the past. The pursuit of knowledge and exploration should be guided by ethical principles and a commitment to the betterment of humanity.

Questions for Reflection:

1.	How do Nostradamus's prophecies about exploration resonate with current scientific and technological advancements?

2.	What are the potential benefits and risks of exploring new frontiers, both on Earth and in space?

3.	How can we ensure that human exploration is conducted in a responsible and sustainable manner, respecting the environment and the rights of indigenous peoples?

As we stand on the threshold of a new era of exploration, Nostradamus's prophecies serve as a reminder of the boundless potential of human curiosity and the enduring allure of the unknown. The future of exploration is in our hands, and it is up to us to shape it with wisdom, courage, and a deep respect for the wonders of our universe.

CHAPTER 100: REFLECTING ON NOSTRADAMUS IN 2024: A LEGACY OF MYSTERY AND INTRIGUE

As 2024 draws to a close, the enigmatic prophecies of Nostradamus continue to captivate and perplex. The year has been filled with a cascade of events, both foreseen and unforeseen, leaving us to ponder the enduring relevance of the 16th-century seer's cryptic verses. This final chapter serves as a retrospective, examining the accuracy and relevance of Nostradamus's predictions for 2024, the enduring appeal of prophecy in shaping human expectations, and the tantalizing prospect of future predictions yet to be unveiled.

The Enigma of Accuracy: A Retrospective Analysis

The year 2024 has been a tumultuous one, marked by significant political, economic, and environmental upheavals. While some of these events seemed to align with Nostradamus's prophecies, others took us by surprise, underscoring the inherent difficulty of interpreting his enigmatic verses.

For instance, Quatrain II.62, which speaks of a "great drought" and "fires from the sky," could be seen as a foreshadowing of the devastating wildfires that ravaged parts of Europe and North America in 2024. However, the quatrain's mention of a "change of reign" and a "new king" did not materialize in the literal sense, highlighting the subjective nature of interpretation and the potential for confirmation bias.

Similarly, Quatrain X.72, which predicts a "great earthquake" and a "change of reign," could be linked to the political instability and social unrest witnessed in several countries during 2024. However, the quatrain's specific references to London and a "pestilence in Tuscany" did not come to pass, underscoring the limitations of prophecy as a precise predictor of events.

The Enduring Appeal of Prophecy

Despite the ambiguities and uncertainties surrounding Nostradamus's predictions, his prophecies continue to captivate audiences worldwide. The allure of peering into the future, even if through a clouded lens, is a testament to the enduring human fascination with the unknown.

Throughout history, prophecies have played a significant role in shaping human expectations and actions. They have inspired hope, instilled fear, and sparked movements for social and political change. The power of prophecy lies not necessarily in its accuracy but in its ability to ignite our imaginations and challenge us to think beyond the present moment.

Nostradamus's prophecies, with their cryptic language and evocative imagery, have inspired countless interpretations and debates, spanning centuries and continents. The fact that we are still discussing them today, over 450 years after they were written, is a testament to their enduring power and relevance.

Looking Forward: The Next Century of Prophecies

As we look towards the future, Nostradamus's prophecies continue to beckon us with their tantalizing glimpses of what might be. While his predictions for 2024 may not have unfolded exactly as some interpreters anticipated, the possibility of future prophecies coming to pass remains open.

It is important to remember that Nostradamus's quatrains are not meant to be read as literal predictions but rather as symbolic representations of potential futures. They invite us to engage in critical thinking, to question our assumptions about the world, and to consider the possible consequences of our actions.

As we move forward, it is crucial to approach Nostradamus's prophecies with a healthy dose of scepticism and a commitment to rational inquiry. By analysing his verses in the context of historical and cultural trends, we can gain valuable insights into the challenges and opportunities that lie ahead.

In the end, the true value of Nostradamus's prophecies lies not in their ability to predict the future, but in their power to inspire reflection, spark dialogue, and encourage us to envision a better world. Whether we believe in the literal truth of his verses or not, their enduring legacy reminds us of the importance of hope, resilience, and the human capacity for transformation.